Walk Softly With Me:

Adventures of a Woman Big-Game Guide In Alaska

T0164327

Sharon E. McLeod-Everette

Printed in Canada
First edition 1998

Elmer E. Rasmuson Library Cataloging-in-Publication Data

McLeod-Everette, Sharon E.
Walk softly with me: adventures of a woman big-game guide in Alaska/Sharon
E. McLeod-Everette.

p. cm.

1. Hunting guides—Alaska—Biography.   2. Big game hunting—Alaska.
3. McLeod-Everette, Sharon E.   I. Title.

SK49.M35 1998

ISBN 0-940055-50-3

Photos by the author unless otherwise credited.
Design and layout by Sue Mitchell, Inkworks
Map and cover design by Russell C. Mitchell

Table of Contents

Guiding big-game hunters is obviously no longer the sole realm of males. Sharon McLeod-Everette guides with skill, tact, and respect for our great north country, its wondrous wildlife, and her diverse clientele. She weaves the tale of her adventures with the same skill and devotion.

—Pete Buist, Alaska Master Guide

"In clear, honest language, Sharon McLeod-Everette brings out the best and sometimes the worst in her experiences as one of Alaska's few woman big game guides. Her eye for detail is excellent, whether she is telling a good hunting story or recollecting her life on an Alaskan homestead in the fifties. Through her writing, I come to appreciate the strength of her good humor and good cheer. Together they make Walk Softly With Me *a joy and pleasure to read."*

—Frank Soos, Professor of English, University of Alaska Fairbanks

Acknowledgements

My deepest thanks to my husband Michael, my mother, sisters, and their families; guides Pete Buist, Wayne Hanson, and Mike Tinker; hunters and friends Don Cameron, Babe Evans, Melissa Jones, John Musacchia, Dale Ruth, and Don Wanie; professors Eric Heyne, Janis Lull, and John Murray (my graduate school advising committee), and to fellow writers in my professional writing group: Carlene Bowne, Kathy Dubbs, Sharon Kessey, Rosalie L'Ecuyer, Sue Mitchell, Joni McNutt, Dan Solie, and Martha Springer, for their professional and caring reading and comments.

Walk Softly With Me

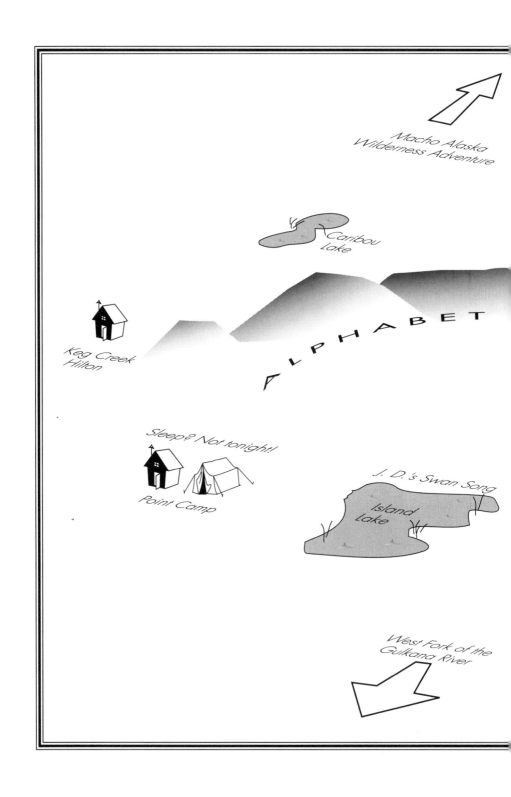

Macho Alaska
Wilderness Adventure

Caribou
Lake

ALPHABET

Keg Creek
Hilton

Sleep? Not tonight!

Point Camp

J. D.'s Swan Song
Island
Lake

West Fork of the
Gulkana River

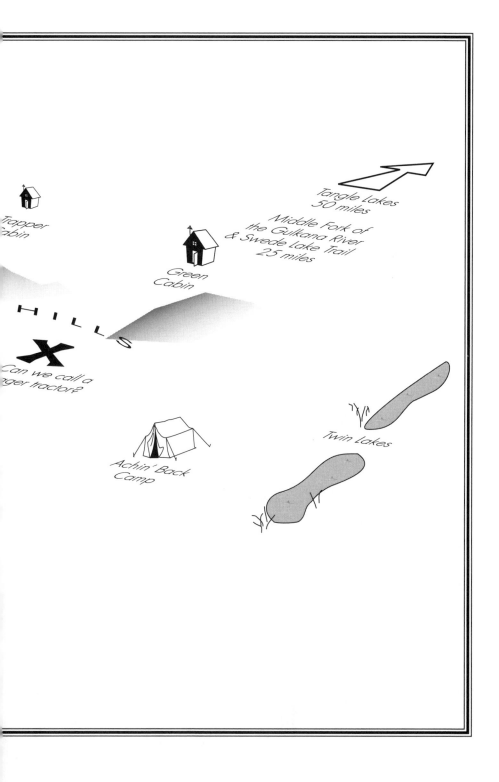

The Beginning of a Hunting Life

*I've lived amidst plenty and have pursued an avocation that led
me to spend much time in the wilderness...I have been witness to
dramas of the wild that are forever taking place—many that the
average person never sees.*

Ernest F. "Fee" Hellman, *Kootenay Country*

THE ROOTS OF MY HUNTING and guiding life took hold a long time ago. I
guess you'd say the seed came north when I was an eight-month-old baby:
my parents and I left Michigan, headed for Alaska to homestead. After a
three-month trip with one major breakdown (lost the rear end on the truck) and
a few flat tires over the primitive, all-dirt and just-opened Alcan, we arrived in
the Territory of Alaska. We settled in a very rural area along the Glenn Highway
in August 1950, a month before my first birthday.

By choosing to homestead in the freedom that territorial Alaska offered, Mother
and Daddy unknowingly charted a course of independence and resilience for
their daughters, Roberta and Sue and me. We learned that when others told us
"no, it's not possible" or "you can't do that" it often meant we could still do it, if
we chose to overcome the obstacles littering the way. Our parents' confidence in
us instilled the belief that we could do just about anything we set our minds to.
Their fortitude and ability to roll through life's headlong twists and turns into
good and bad taught us that we could survive anything and come up laughing.

We also learned to accept all different kinds of people: missionaries, roadhouse owners, cat-skinners, teachers, alcoholics, Athabaskans, Eskimos, people
from the United States,[1] traveling salesmen, hermits, and crooks. In our young
minds, they got categorized into groups: The Mission, The Copper Valley School
People, The Alaska Road Commission camp, The Alaska Communications System camp, Fish and Wildlife, Copper Center People, Gakona People, Gulkana
People, The School Teachers, The Traveling Public Health Nurses, and The People
We Never Saw Again, to name some. Probably because so few people lived in the
Copper River Valley, we thought anybody was good company, quirks or not.

One man, good-natured as could be, was a little off because of time spent in a Nazi concentration camp—you could see the blue numbers tattooed on his wrist. He made his own bolts, hacksawing metal rods for hours; he also built a track rig out of a wringer-washing machine motor, leftover parts from odds and ends of cannibalized pickups, and broken tracks from a Weasel[2] that others had given up on. There were several people like him: mentally different, but kind and harmless. It was okay to have them over for dinner. Other people were criminals, and a sixth sense would tell us not to be too friendly. When they stopped by to visit, their eyes would rove all over the interior of our house and they would ask too many questions. Mendeltna Lodge, twelve miles away, housed a stripping and refurbishing branch of a car-theft ring headquartered in Florida; they were caught after about six months. It was also the short-term home of a man who murdered his wife, chopped her in pieces, and partially burned the remains in the fireplace. Then he put them in a barrel and took the barrel to the Mendeltna dump. He didn't get away with it.

My sisters and I grew up on our 158-acre homestead with just a few neighbors. We were 25 miles from Glennallen, the nearest settlement, and 164 miles from Anchorage, the closest metropolitan center. Neighbors included a family a quarter mile up the road to the east, and another across the road. Both had followed us up the Alcan once we reported back to Michigan that land could, indeed, be homesteaded. The family across the road gave way a few short years later to Bill and Queenie Bourdeau, a retired couple from New York who were the parents and in-laws of the White family who ran Atlasta House, a roadhouse two miles east on the Glenn Highway. The growing family at Atlasta House included John and Marcy and their children: Paul, who is my age; Clare, who is Roberta's age; and later, Gene and Marie, who bracketed Sue in age.

Another neighbor was Tex Smith, owner of Trapper's Den, another lodge two miles to the west. Tex had the distinction of being the father of Perry Smith, one of the murderers in Truman Capote's book, *In Cold Blood.* Perry, who lived with his father for a time, babysat Roberta and me once or twice. He gave us a black motorcycle seat ringed with shiny metal studs and big metal handles on each side of the back. Our imaginations, the saddle, and a tipped-over fifty-five gallon drum took us galloping on horseback or spinning gravel on wild motorcycle rides.

Trapper's Den changed hands over the years, with different families of varied, colorful, and sometimes lawless lifestyles inhabiting the place. It was also vacant for long periods of time.

Al and Helen Lee and their two children, Tricia and Jerry, moved in six miles away and opened up a guide service. Tazlina Glacier Lodge, open year-round and owned by Glen and Celia Griffin, was ten miles to the west on Smokey Lake. On the other side of the lake, two half-brothers, Chuck Sutter and Lloyd

Ronning, ran hunting and fishing guiding services. Morrie and Joe Secondchief, and Joe's brothers Jimmie and Dick, lived in their individual log cabins on the Glennallen side of Mendeltna. Morrie and Joe opened their home to Sunday school classes and church services; folks from the Central Alaska Mission drove from Glennallen, picked us up on the way, and did the services in Morrie and Joe's two-room log cabin. Music came from a foot-pump portable organ.

Mendeltna Lodge attracted the same kind of occupants as Trapper's Den. A few people lived farther away in both directions, and other families slowly moved in as time passed. Today, the area is more heavily populated. Families live about

Roberta McLeod (rear) and the author, riding a barrel while sitting on Perry Smith's motorcycle seat—1955.

two miles apart along a thirty-mile stretch of highway, and more people have built across the road from each other. Some subdivisions with plots of five to ten acres even exist, so three or more families live less than a mile from each other, with their driveways T-ing off the subdivision road.

Roberta, three years younger than me, was born in our living room, just outside Mother and Daddy's bedroom. The delivery bed was next to the green, fake-leather-covered boot bench attached to the wall that separated living room from bedroom. The bedroom was just large enough for a double bed; a dresser made to match the walls, all from the honey-blonde spruce milled from our sawmill; an aluminum-pipe clothes-hanging rod against the interior wall that backed the hall closet; and a two-foot by four-foot window facing the road. A clothes closet formed the wall between Mother and Daddy's bedroom and the kids' bedroom—if you opened the closet doors in one bedroom, you could crawl through the closet and exit in the other bedroom, as long as the doors on that side weren't latched. Only a bare bulb gave light, when the gasoline power plant was running. The living room, on the other hand, was three and a half times bigger than the bedroom. It also had much more natural light, with two paned picture windows and two the same size as the one bedroom window. The two beam-mounted electric light fixtures held four bulbs each. Two two-mantle Coleman lamps, one on each side of the barrel stove centered in the living room, gave us light to read by when the power plant wasn't running, which was most of the time. The Colemans hung from a hook in the middle of a piece of metal, which was cut from a Blazo can and suspended from the ceiling by bolts at each corner, so the heat from the lanterns wouldn't catch the house on fire.

We didn't have a phone. Daddy had to go to Atlasta House so he could call Dr. Chester Schneider at Central Alaska Missions in Glennallen to let him know the baby was on its way, and that he should be on his way to our house. Dr. Chet, as he was more affectionately known, had to come to our house to do the delivery, because the mission had no hospital.

A gentleman and his wife, Vincent J. and Beckie Joy, started Central Alaska Missions in the Copper River Basin in the mid-forties, with a few small churches here and there, either in someone's house or a specially built small log cabin. Soon, the mission hired Dr. Schneider, built a hospital and hired another doctor, Dr. Jim Pinneo. Today, a radio station and the Alaska Bible College are part of the mission, because Vince Joy had the ability to dream and to believe in his dreams. An excellent hospital existed for around thirty years, until insurance requirements drove it out of business. Now there's only a clinic.

Roberta's birth was a big enough occasion that the gasoline power plant was running to provide electricity, and neighbors filled the kitchen. They woke me up to tell me I had a new baby sister. I don't recall much, except that the too-bright bare light bulbs hanging from the kitchen ceiling hurt my eyes, the whole house was deafeningly noisy, and I had to go potty. All the people carrying me around on their shoulders kept forgetting to take me to the thundermug (a metal, porcelain-covered potty-bucket) in the bathroom.

Sue, nine years younger, was born in Central Alaska Mission's Faith Hospital in Glennallen, a few years after it opened. I remember waking up in the wee hours of the morning to Mother sleeping on our living room couch. When I shook her shoulder, I was shocked to discover that it actually belonged to Billy, Bill and Queenie's middle-aged son. Billy was there to take care of me and Roberta while Mother was rushed off to the new hospital in the middle of the night to have Sue. Whatever I had wanted promptly deserted me, and I dashed back to bed.

We thought everyone lived life the way we and all the locals did—working hard and playing harder. It didn't occur to us girls that our stateside relatives thought we lived beyond the reaches of civilization. To them, we were pioneers in a last frontier, living in the wild, deprived of all sorts of niceties like running water, fully functional indoor bathrooms, and electricity. Our ranging knew only the bounds of how far away we could get and still be back before lunch or dinner, constrained only by the number of chores that had to be done. It took all of us to haul wood and water, keep the garden, split wood for the kitchen cookstove and the living room barrel-stove, stack the wood, do laundry with a wringer-washer on washday, and keep up with regular daily dishes. Because they were the equipment that was our lifeline, we kept the pickup, the Ford Ferguson tractor, the Cletrac (a small dozer), and the Weasel in good repair. And we had schoolwork, when we were old enough. First, Mother taught us correspondence courses, sent to us by the Territorial Department of Education, which contracted with Calvert Course out of Baltimore, Maryland. Then, when a school was built in Glennallen and there were enough students to warrant it, we had a three-seater station wagon school bus to carry us on the fifty-mile round trip.

We learned, too, about guns and their purpose, and were taught how to shoot early in life. So early, in fact, I can't even remember learning how. Red squirrels with a penchant for swiping our house-log chinking and for infuriating Buzzy, our dog, made for an endless supply of target practice.

In the late fifties, Daddy smashed his left wrist in a summer work accident, a disaster not only because he was left-handed, but also because he had to have pins put in his wrist and was in a cast up to his shoulder all winter. The Euclid belly-dump rolled as a soft shoulder of the Denali Highway (under construction at the time) gave way, and the belly-dump's 200-pound battery tumbled out, landing on his left wrist. He couldn't hunt the fall or winter moose season, and somehow we had to get enough food to last a year. There weren't any stores around, and even if there were, I don't think we could have afforded the price of meat. Mother shot an autumn caribou and when that ran out, Roberta and I shot and snared snowshoe hares to supplement the canned salmon that had to last us through the winter. We ate rabbit after rabbit after rabbit.

Rabbit detail was sandwiched between our regular winter chores of chopping firewood for the kitchen stove and splitting larger pieces of wood for the living room's barrel stove. It was woven into the daily pattern of filling the indoor woodboxes, hauling water, and snow-shovelling. Snow-shovelling was more than just clearing paths to the woodpiles and the garage, and the entire driveway so the pickup could get out. It also meant filling box after box the size of Xerox-paper cases with snow and tobogganing them to the house. The boxes of snow got poured into copper boilers on the stoves to make clothes-washing water for laundry day and for bath and shampoo water. And we spent hours on snowshoes with the .22 rifle, checking snares, collecting rabbits.

The rabbits in the snares were usually frozen, so we stacked them cordwood-style outside the house. We'd bring one in, string it upside down over the kitchen sink (the rabbit-skinning nail is still there in the beam), let it thaw a bit, and peel the hide off, the guts coming with it. The cats loved rabbit-skinning time, purring and winding around Mother's legs. Not only were they trained to the smell of rabbit, they also knew the sound of the butcher knife being sharpened. Then, they would come at full meow, skidding into the kitchen. The sound of stone against knife meant scraps for them.

Bruce McLeod with his broken wrist, flanked by Roberta, right, and the author. Myrtle McLeod's caribou rack is atop the pickup canopy.

Mother was creative in the cooking department, but ingenuity only lasted so many days before rabbit repeats showed up. Rabbits for breakfast, lunch, and dinner. Rabbit and rice. Stewed, with dumplings, with mashed potatoes; fried, with fried potatoes; in soups with vegetables. Stewed, with pancakes. Stewed, with oatmeal. Stewed or fried, with or without gravy. Ugh. The year of the rabbit is indelibly filed in the family memory bank, but had us kids not learned to shoot and hunt, we would have had an even leaner winter. The moose we lacked that year would have been ground up and pressure-canned for hamburger patties, spaghetti, chili, and meat loaf, or chunked up and pressure-canned for stews and stroganoff. We also could have had roasts, and ribs to barbecue in the pressure cooker. We were very happy when Daddy's wrist healed enough to allow him to hunt again.

Back then, we shot two large moose (or three when Bill hunted too)—one during the first season in the autumn, and another in the second season during the often bitter cold of winter. The early moose was chunked or burgered and then pressure-sealed in quart Kerr and Mason jars. The November moose hung in the meathouse, quartered and frozen. We brought a quarter indoors when we ran low on fresh meat. The quarter hung over the double laundry tub on wheels in Roberta's and my bedroom (where it was stored between laundry days) so blood wouldn't drip on the floor. When it thawed, we butchered it into roasts, steaks, and stew meat. Then we wrapped the pieces in butcher paper or waxed paper and newspaper and put them back outside in the five-gallon, blue-and-white Crisco shortening cans that were stashed in the snow banked up against the house like a freezer condo. All you had to do was step outside to the condo bank to get the main course for dinner.

It took two large moose to feed us and Bill and Queenie. Roberta, Sue, and I had adopted them as grandparents. We never had the opportunity to meet our own grandparents; Daddy's parents died when he was young, and Mother's died before I was out of my teens. Bill and Queenie had seen hard times during the Depression and, like our parents, subscribed to the theory that you had to be self-sufficient and able to laugh at yourself. The stories they told on themselves, with gales of laughter and a New York accent, made an impression on us.

Sometimes in the summer the Athabaskans Daddy worked with on the Alaska Road Commission road maintenance crew would loan us a fishwheel for a night. We'd fill the back of our half-ton blue Chevrolet pickup with salmon—we'd be up all night, hauling fish by hand from the basket of the wheel, carrying them across an often-rickety, three-pole-wide aspen bridge over a channel of the Copper River, to the pickup. Us kids fell asleep on the thirty-mile drive home.

Then came the fish cleaning and canning process, and smoking some of the fish. Two days later, we'd get to bed, dizzy and dead on our feet. The men cleaned while Mother and Queenie cut the fish in pieces small enough to fit through the mouths of the quart and half-quart Mason jars and then stuffed the jars three-quarters full, adding seasonings and water. Some fish were cut in strips and sent back outdoors to the men to brine and prepare for the smokehouse. Two Coleman stoves and two huge pressure cookers would run indoors until the canning job was done. Roberta and I had three main jobs—wash the glass jars and metal lids with steaming-hot water to sterilize them, help Mother and Queenie pack the jars with salmon strips and chunks, screw on the two-part lids, and then time the cookers, keeping a sharp eye on the pressure gauges. Too much pressure would blow up the cooker, scald us, and who knew what else. Fortunately, we never experienced that nightmare. We monitored the stoves and cookers with an alertness governed by fear. The first fear was of the pain of being burned by suddenly released steam, and the second was the thought of our home going up in flames from the Coleman stoves and white gas that we would surely tip over in such an emergency. Plus the idea of scrubbing away the mushy salmon that would have stuck to the rough-hewn ship-lap walls sounded like way too much work, in case the house didn't burn down.

Left: the author with Roberta McLeod and Queenie Bourdeau (holding a rifle and a porcupine) with Buzzy the dog.

Right: Bruce McLeod grinding moose into burger. The grinder has been adapted by replacing the hand crank with a flywheel, powered by a pulley run off the Ford Ferguson tractor power take-off unit.

We played as much as we worked—maybe more, because doing chores became a contest, and we always gabbed while we worked. Roberta and I would see who could split the most wood, carry the biggest armload of kitchen stove wood, or throw the most rocks out of the garden. We pedaled balloon-tired bicycles as fast as we could on the road or through the bushes on trails around the homestead. We played catch with the dishrag instead of doing dishes—until we got caught.

I began my "guiding" at an early age, probably earlier than was healthy for my parents. Somewhere around age three, I convinced Raymond, the kid across the road, that I knew where his mother had gone to pick blueberries, and that we could find her. Several hours later, they found us half a mile up the road and way off in the bushes. Somewhere in our wanderings, Raymond and I saw a black bear. With me around, the wandering neighbor who enticed their children into getting lost in the wilderness, it's no wonder those parents chose to return to Michigan.

Another sojourn found me leading Paul, the boy from Atlasta House, off into the forest south of our house on some of the logging trails. I remember being lost then, and I remember finding my way back home. I also remember getting in trouble.

"Little terrors" probably describes Roberta and me pretty accurately, although we didn't think so then. We dreamed up activities to occupy ourselves, as most kids do. It's just that we chose odd things to do, things that our parents didn't know about until years later, and even then they blanched at what we'd done. Saying they were angry at us is an understatement.

Roberta and I used to stretch out on our stomachs on the centerline of the two-lane highway, foot-to-foot, waiting for a car to come. There wasn't much traffic in those days, so we soaked up the warmth from the gray asphalt (obviously a summertime activity) and talked lazily while we waited. Although we watched for cars, we listened more, keeping an ear on the pavement. Sometimes it would be half an hour or more before we would hear a car or truck off in the distance. When a car got close (we deemed a hundred yards to be close), whichever one of us was responsible for the direction the car was coming from would yell, and we'd scramble up and run, often without looking at the car. We raced to opposite sides of the road, disappearing into the bushes amid the screech of brakes and, I'm sure, the cursing of the drivers.

Maybe some reader will remember being startled by two red-headed Orphan Annie look-alikes leaping up from the middle of the road and disappearing into a willow thicket.

But I'm straying from my path. This story is about how hunting and guiding began for me; homesteading is for another time.

School Doesn't Hold a Candle to a First Moose

ALL SUMMER I PRACTICED shooting. It was 1963; I was thirteen, going on fourteen. Daddy started me out on the 30.06, one of his old military rifles. Mahogany brown and smooth to the touch, the 30.06 had open iron sights. Back then, most of the local people considered scopes to be a frippery. Scopes weren't as well made as they are today, so they fogged up too easily. Besides, open sights worked just fine since most of our shots were a hundred yards or less and in pretty brushy country.

After a few years of shooting a .22 rifle, the 30.06 was easy to deal with. It was a little heavier, but I was strong. Hauling and chopping wood and keeping up with our other chores made my sisters and me tougher than most kids our age, boys or girls. Even Sue, who was much younger and spent only her first five years without electricity and oil-fired heat, was far stronger than she looked.

"This fall, we'll see if we can't get you your first moose," Daddy said. "Do your target practice, and remember to *squeeze* the trigger. If you jerk, it'll throw your shot off."

He was proud when he saw most of the shots in the black on the target. "No moose will get away from you!" he exclaimed.

Because he worked all week for the Highway Department, we reserved the weekends for making trips back into the hills to hunt. On weekdays, we did what everybody else did: got up about 4:30 in the morning and road hunted. Except our road hunting included a lot of gravel-pit-sitting also.

A typical morning would go like this: at 4:30, Daddy would tiptoe into the bedroom I shared with my sister, whisper "Daylight in the swamp," grab my big toe, and shake my foot to be sure I awoke. He had to go for the big toe because I slept in the top part of the trundle bed, and that's all he could reach.

I'd slip into my jeans and flannel shirt and bumble bleary-eyed through our green, chenille-curtained bedroom door into the kitchen where the kerosene Aladdin lamp glowed softly on the kitchen table. He already had a pot of coffee cheerily perking on our propane cookstove. As soon as the coffee was done,

Daddy poured it into a dinged Aladdin thermos for the road. I tried to eat something—toast or cold dinner leftovers from the night before—before we left, but I usually stuffed it into a napkin to munch on as we drove slowly.

Our blue Chevy pickup purred quietly, in concert with its tires crunching on the gravel as we left our driveway. When we turned onto the pavement, the crunching turned to a hum. Morning fog would usually be lifting from the lakes and low-lying swamps as we eased along the highway. The wispy white fog gave an ethereal look to the green, tinged-with-gold areas we passed. I knew my job: inspect my side of the road, hoping to find a moose; look hard to discern moose shapes from dark stumps and misshapen bushes. Daddy would take care of his side of the road. Sometimes we would meet someone coming from the opposite direction; we'd pass with a one-handed salute—or stop in the road for a low-voiced chat. Usually, there was no need to move on for another vehicle because traffic was sparse. The only motivation to drive on was time ticking away, the departure hour for work and school sneaking up.

We had a rote list of gravel pits to get to and slowly search through. In some, there were special parking spots from which to look. At those, we stayed in the pickup. At other gravel pits—those surrounded with brush—we parked, got out, and crawled up an embankment to survey the open fields below. Then we would walk slowly along the top of the embankment from one vantage point to the next, moving from one end of the gravel pit to the other. Sometimes, Daddy would send me back to get the pickup (a big deal for a fourteen-year-old) while he did the last bit of looking; other times, I did the last look while he got the pickup.

By the time we headed home, the sun was a big fireball on the eastern horizon, glowing yellow-orange and making us squint as we drove into it. Dewy green late-summer leaves shimmered and glittered in the slanting morning light; some days, it was cold enough to frost and the sun dampened the white into crystalline drips running off pointed brilliant green or golden leaf ends.

The summer I learned to shoot the big rifle, Daddy assured me that he and I would try for a cow moose and one of last year's calves. (For several years in the sixties, resident hunters were allowed to shoot both cows and bulls.) We road-hunted every day, beginning August 20, opening day.

The first day of school that year was also my fourteenth birthday. The day began just as all other hunting days—up early, roll out of the driveway, ease onto the road. Two things were different, though. Daddy had a very stiff neck, and it was foggier than normal. Daddy's stiff neck meant I had more responsibility for looking since he couldn't turn his head; the fog meant that we passed up some of our regular spots. We agreed that this would be an abbreviated morning, a good thing since it was the first day of school, and I was starting tenth grade. This was the big time—no longer a lowly freshman in high school!

We headed for the White Alice site, a communications repeater station about two miles from home. Run by the Alaska Communications System, a branch of the Air Force, it was a good place for blueberries, lowbush cranberries, spruce grouse, and moose. Staring through the mist didn't make a moose materialize during the two-mile trip up the steep hill. We parked in front of the repeater site gate and walked toward the edge of the bank that faced west.

"Stop," Daddy hissed. I froze.

"Go back to the pickup and get the rifles," he whispered.

I hurried as quietly as I could, reached into the pickup (we never shut the doors—the metallic bang would send animals away), pulled out the 30.06 and the 30.40, and stepped lightly back to where Daddy had crouched.

"Look down there. Tell me what you see," he said quietly.

"I don't see anything," I replied, straining to see through the wispy fog. "Oh, but I hear something!" I added quickly. I had heard the unmistakable thump of animal footfalls, but their location was distorted by the fog.

Then I saw the cow moose. "There, Daddy! There's a cow!" Just as quickly, I saw the young bull with stubby spike antlers that was with her. "Daddy, Daddy, there's a bull too!"

Daddy, stiff neck forgotten, grabbed one of the rifles. He snatched the 30.06, the rifle I had been practicing with. That left me with the 30.40, which I had never shot and which had peep sights rather than open sights.

He aimed, and downed the cow. He stood, watching for the bull to reappear in the drifting mist. While he did that, I tried the sights on the 30.40. I eased the rifle up and aimed at a tree. Lining up the front sight through the round peep-hole of the rear sight seemed pretty easy, so I began to look and listen for the little bull. Daddy was still staring to his right when I saw the shadowy form of the bull off to the left in the willows. I lifted the 30.40, aimed, and squeezed the trigger. The bull crumpled into a pile and Daddy jumped as though I'd jabbed him with a sharp stick.

"Jesus! Why didn't you tell me you were going to shoot? I just twisted my neck again!"

Then he realized I'd shot my first moose—with one shot, no less. And with a rifle I'd never shot before.

"That's my girl! A chip off the old block! Let's go home and get Mother and the knives." We checked both moose to be sure they were dead, and scrambled back to the pickup.

I glowed all the way home. It was my birthday, and I shot my first moose! I was going to stay home from school and clean it.

Fifteen minutes later, my plans were a smoldering heap. Mother and Daddy had other ideas. I wasn't going to miss school. Furthermore, since we needed more moose, I couldn't even tell anybody I'd shot it. If word leaked out that the repeater site was a good moose spot, everybody and his brother would be there—and Mother still had hers to shoot. If there were more moose around, Daddy wanted our family to have first crack at them. After all, we had to feed ourselves all winter, and we had Bill and Queenie to worry about too. Two small moose might do us for the winter, but it didn't leave any extra for Bill and Queenie, or enough to last in case we had a longer winter than normal.

Crestfallen, I cleaned up and changed clothes. I stewed all the way to school. Starting sophomore year was eclipsed by shooting my first moose. I was jumping-in-my-clothes excited and couldn't brag to anybody about it.

I cannot tell you what happened at school that day, but the pent up excitement and feverish desire to tell someone, anyone, that I'd shot my moose are as real today as they were then. To make matters worse, some of the boys were bragging about the moose they were going to get when they went hunting with their fathers.

I bit my tongue.

What I wouldn't have given to have said smugly, "I shot mine this morning, even before school."

So, How'd You Get to Be a Guide?

NEARLY EVERY HUNTING SEASON, I have to explain to new hunters how it is I came to be a guide. They're always curious about my background, particularly when they learn I grew up on a homestead. All of the hunters I've guided have been men, and many of them aren't sure that I can produce what they came to Alaska for. I don't blame them. I'm not a big person, and I don't look strong; they don't know that I exercise all year and play basketball all winter. My voice doesn't always sound authoritative. So I do some explaining, then let my experience do the rest of the talking.

Our hunters know ahead of time that Tangle Lakes Outfitters (once misheard as Tangled Legs Outfitters—appropriate for pucker-brush walking) and Hanson Enterprises have a lady guide, and we ask if they have a problem being placed with a woman. The answer is always no.

But when they arrive at the lake where I meet them with the Bombardier, and Wayne Hanson, experienced pilot, guide, and incredibly accomplished handyman, lifts his floatplane into the air to fetch their remaining gear and hunting partner, their smiles inevitably fade. Their conversation turns uneasy and strained. Self-consciousness creeps into their voices and actions, and I can see sidelong glances aimed my direction as I clean tracks on the Bombardier, make lists of supplies for Wayne to bring on a return trip, and do general camp maintenance.

Wayne, whom they've just flown in with, and I are about the same size, standing five feet eight inches. We both have blue eyes and laugh a lot, but the similarity ends there. He's a man, I'm a woman. His hair is nearly white, mine is red with salt beginning to mix in; his Levis cover angular hips, mine cover rounded ones. He looks tough and wiry; I don't.

Often, the hunters have also met two other guides of Clearwater Outdoor Services: Pete Buist, who occasionally helps out, and Mike Tinker, Wayne's partner. Pete, Tinker, and I, Fairbanksans who often spend moose seasons together, are probably an odd-looking crew. Long-legged Pete, easily six feet five inches, takes one stride to my two, stepping blithely over pucker-brush that I struggle through. What you see through a pair of binoculars as he leads someone my size on a stalk is Pete in slow motion amble followed by hunter at high-speed trot.

Tinker is a six-foot bundle of compact energy who is so effective at stalking and calling moose that he's had a cow moose come up to sniff the brim of his cap. I appear as their perfect foil: red-haired, freckle-faced, and shorter.

Completely at home in the woods, I am accustomed to waiting the few days that hunters need to get used to a woman guide. I'm sure the hunters are apprehensive because they've invested so much money in this once-in-a-lifetime opportunity. They have no idea where they are. There's no intersection of Fourth and Main here, and no way to know which trail leads out. Even north is disguised because Alaska's magnetic declination is skewed due to our northwesterly place on the globe. They're also afraid I won't pull through for them, and they're not sure if I can field-dress such a large animal as a moose. Some have emotional baggage to accompany the monetary consideration. They've boasted about their hunting prowess and how they're going to come back with an Alaska moose. They wonder if a woman can help them find it. Is she strong enough to field-dress it and take care of the meat?

Their questions spill over, beginning as the men arrive at Island Lake one by one. They sit lakeside in the warm morning sun watching the loons float past,

The author with fellow guide Pete Buist in 1991 up the Johnson River, hunting grizzly bears in 75-degree weather.

waiting for the other Cessna-loads of their gear and partners. And glancing quiz-zically at me as if I've betrayed some cardinal rule that says only crusty men with beards can be guides. Their faces clearly say that they view me as exactly what I am: an anomaly in the male-dominated guiding world.

These hunters, here for the second half of the September moose season in Game Management Unit 13B, are very similar to most who come to hunt with our small cadre of guides and assistant guides. They are awed and a little intimi-dated by the vast expanses of uninhabited land, astonished by the thousands of small ponds and lakes that they saw dappling the landscape on their flight here. Breathing deeply of the achingly clear air, they remark at the crystalline quality of the sharply blue sky and the searing whiteness of the rugged Wrangells in the distance.

The men ask questions to prompt me to describe how I got into hunting. I talk as I continue to pump up the fuel tank on the Coleman stove. Our moose-stew lunch has been cooking, and the flame under the pot looks low.

"I've hunted all my life. In fact, I grew up on a homestead about fifty miles east, cross country from where we're hunting now. From the top of that hill above camp," I point, "on a clear night you can see the light from the microwave repeater site that's two miles from my mother's house." Usually, I forget to tell them it's also where I shot my first moose.

I go on, explaining that hunting was critical for our family. We didn't have electricity or running water, and we lived 164 miles from the nearest town. So we shopped only once a year for dried and canned goods and fresh vegetables and meat. We used an ice-box refrigerator as long as there was ice, but fresh vegetables and meat didn't last too long. We didn't shop for large quantities of those things. At least not in the traditional sense—our "shopping" was done in the garden with seeds, rake, and hoe . . . and in the forest with rifles.

"How did you keep warm?" asks a freckle-faced, sandy-haired hunter. Crinkles at the corners of his eyes give him the look of someone who enjoys smiling, but the furrows in his brow speak volumes about work pressures. Or so I assume.

"We used wood for both the kitchen cookstove and the barrel stove in the living room. What they say about cutting wood really is true. It warms you about six times over before you ever get to burning it," I respond.

"Why do you say that?"

I ask one of them to stir the stew so it doesn't stick to the bottom of the pot. My hands are filled with dishes and silverware as I arrange the meal in an assem-bly line so we can fill our bowls with food, get hot coffee, and butter our bread.

"That's kind of an old homesteader's saying," I continue. "The first warming comes when you cut down the trees; the second is when you chop all the limbs off. Then you have to cut it up in sections small enough to carry by hand or haul by some means. Once you get it home, you have to cut it up into stove-length pieces, and then you have to split it. Stacking it warms you up; so does hauling it into the house."

Their questions remind me of my family's weekend wood-hauling and chopping duties, and I grimace. "I'm glad we finally got electricity."

"How did you get around?" This hunter worked in the construction business.

"We had a 1950 Chevy pickup. Mostly, Daddy used it for going to work. There wasn't anywhere for Mother and us kids to go even if there had been another car. Glennallen, the closest little community, is twenty-five miles away, and our nearest neighbors were close enough to walk to."

"How cold does it get here in the winter?"

"Oh, where I grew up, the coldest it's ever been is about forty degrees below zero—Farenheit, not Celsius. Glennallen gets a lot colder. Most winters, school would be closed for about a week 'cause it would be sixty below or colder there. At our house, though, it would only be twenty below. We thought we lived in the banana belt."

"If you didn't have electricity, how did you keep your pickup running when it got too cold? Did you just have to park it for the winter?" One man poses the questions, but seems to be asking for all of them. They are familiar with equipment, and can't imagine dealing with the cold without electricity and garages.

Left: The author (right) and her sister Roberta haul wood for the kitchen cook-stove in 1956 or 1957.

Right: The author at age 2 ½ with her father, Bruce McLeod.

"No, we didn't park it. Daddy still needed to go to work—he was an equipment operator for the Alaska Road Commission at the Glennallen shop—and the pickup had to be ready to go in case there was an emergency. When Daddy got home from work, we'd just drain the oil out and bring it in the house for the night. We brought in the battery, too. Then we'd put 'em back in every morning. My job was to have the oil pan, battery strap, and wrenches ready and to hold the flashlight while Daddy took the stuff out. I'd run to open the door to the house so he could carry it all in. Then in the morning the routine was reversed, and we put the oil and battery back in. To warm up the rear end and transmission, we'd use a propane weed burner. You know—a torch. We'd stick it in a stovepipe with a ninety-degree elbow to direct the heat right under the gearbox. Then we'd move it along so the driveline would warm up too."

"What a job! The hunters shake their heads. "You had to do that every day?"

"Every day that it was below zero."

They are also curious about how many other people lived in the area.

"Houses were spaced pretty far apart—four of 'em in a four-mile stretch. One family didn't stay too long, though. Beyond that, the nearest family in each direction was six miles away."

The hunters show interest and growing respect as I tell them more about living on the homestead. Because we lived miles from anyone else, we rarely used babysitters. As a result, our parents took us everywhere, including hunting. I tell them about the game our resourceful mother had devised to keep us occupied and interested when we were young.

"All right, girls. Are you ready to get your eyes focused for moose?" she'd say.

"Ready, Mum," we would chorus.

"Okay, hands up to your eyes. Now, turn 'em back and forth, like this, until you're in focus." She demonstrated. "Got it?"

We'd make circles with our fingers, put them up in front of our eyes and turn them left and right like we were adjusting binoculars. And it worked. We always saw moose. Mother's ever-ready wit and ability to turn anything into entertainment helped to make hunting fun.

Daddy, always in his red-and-black checked Woolrich jacket, taught us by example how to walk softly, even on autumn's crinkly yellow carpet of fallen leaves and brown, crisped twigs. Even with his lanky frame and long legs, each footfall was soft and even. His eyes were quick to see the animals, his ears completely attuned to the sounds of the wild. We learned the rapid thump of rabbits' feet drumming, the drawn-out swishing and cracking sounds of a moose walking through brush, and the grunts and moans they used. We also came to distinguish the machine-gun chitters of a disturbed squirrel tattling on whoever or whatever had disturbed it from the nervous, more shrill chatter followed by prolonged, too-still silence that meant "danger!" Daddy showed us the areas moose frequented and how to pick out body shapes from the forest they melded into. Years later, we discovered he had indelibly instilled in us a respect for the animals we pursued and for the land we lived on. If we didn't take care of the animals and the land, they wouldn't take care of us.

Because the craft of hunting was second nature to us, it never occurred to us that people in towns didn't go into the woods to shoot their own animals. We were no more familiar with grocery stores and cash registers than city people were with bagging their own dinner for a year in one fell swoop. It's like having grown up eating turkey, bread-cube dressing, and mashed potatoes with gravy as part of a traditional Thanksgiving feast. If that's what you've done all your life, it's impossible to imagine that other people might have ham, cornbread stuffing, and sweet potatoes or prime rib, baked potato, and a salad.

For my family, like many others who depended on the land for food, hunting was a job. We hunted with focus and intensity, driven by the knowledge that our full year's meat rested directly on our own skills. Although we admired huge antlers, we didn't scrutinize moose for them. Instead, we looked for good, tender bodies. Not babies, but not monsters either. In years when there were cow seasons, we shot those instead of a bull—cow moose have no rutting hormones to make the meat taste strong.

Becoming a guide forced me to add different perspectives to my ideas about what constituted a good hunt. A moose was no longer just tender dinners; antler size became a new focus. Some hunters are interested in one thing—a trophy to land their name in a record book or to make everyone back home envious. Some of the big-antler variety of hunters prefer to sign their meat over to the guides or the crew rather than pay for shipping it home. Some foreign countries don't allow importation of unprocessed meat or of wild game. That's fine with me. I go home with meat, and the moose that otherwise would have been my dinners is free to roam for another year. I admit to the thrill of the challenge of successfully stalking and bagging a trophy animal with a client, and hunting stories captivate me by the hour. But I don't like listening to excessive bragging about trophies from past hunts, when my early family focus was on food for the table and respect for the animal.

Hunters who talk freely of the poaching they do back home astonish me—illegal hunting evidently happens far more than I was aware. I lose respect for "sportsmen" when they brag about how many fish over the limit they got, how they pulled the wool over the game warden's eyes about how many deer they shot, or that they shot two because they saw a bigger one after they shot a little one. Sometimes they suggest that the airplane ought to point out a moose for us, or that I consider shooting the moose for them, and they could just stay in the cabin. I'm nice about it, but they get a short lesson on Alaska's laws and my desire to keep my license. I make certain they know I think hunting should be fair chase—for the hunter and the animal—and that's how my camp operates.

Other hunters, excited and thrilled to be there, are full of questions about wildlife, vegetation, birds, the weather. They own the art of outdoor appreciation, and the hunt quickly becomes much more than a trophy quest for us.

I always wonder how each group of hunters will feel about fair chase and hunting ethics. Are they set on a trophy, or on a good experience? One thing is certain: I'll know by the time the ten-day hunt is over.

Once their curiosity about my family's homesteading is satisfied, the hunters turn back to guiding. "What got you started working for this outfit?" and "How did you meet Mike Tinker and Wayne Hanson?" are frequent questions.

"I've known Tinker since 1966, and he introduced me to Wayne. He and Wayne are partners now; Tinker did his assistant guide work with him, just as I've done mine with the two of them. You've met Wayne, but I don't know if you got to meet Tinker."

"No," one of them responds, "we didn't, but we flew over his camp on the way over here from the lodge at Tangles. We talked to him a lot on the phone to set this trip up. What direction is he from where we are now?"

I turn and point to the right of an abrupt hill that wears a line of yellow-foliaged aspen like a Mohawk haircut. "He has the other Bombardier at a camp called Achin' Back, about fifteen miles northeast of here."

Another hunter, the gregarious ringleader of the group, wants to get back to guiding.

"I gotta hear how this lady got to be a guide. She cooks good; we know that from the tasty moose stew she whipped up."

Heads pivot back toward me.

"How'd you start doing this?"

"A long time ago, it must have been about 1977 or '78, I started coming down to Tangles, taking vacation time from my job to help out with cooking and running the base camp. Mostly, it was a good break from my work. And I got to eat moose and talk hunting with everybody who came through. What I liked best was sitting up late, cozy around the warm barrel stove, listening to great yarns of hunts full of predicaments and good times. You get Wayne and Tinker and some of the old-timers who come every year going and you can really hear some tales. Like how bad the Bombardier got stuck, and when Dale had to spend the night out by himself about a half mile from camp 'cause a snowstorm caught him."

"Well, if you started out cooking, how did you get into the guiding end of the business? Isn't that kind of a big leap?"

"I guess it seems that way. One year—must have been 1982 or '83—Wayne and Tinker had a lot of hunters scheduled to be in camp out here. In fact, it was at the very camp you'll be at. They decided they wanted a cook to go along so the guide didn't have to do everything. I went in with Tinker and Dale Ruth (Dale is one of our repeat hunters and is a reference for prospective hunters; these men had called him) in the Bombardier a few days before opening day to get the camps set up. As it turned out, I did a lot more than just cook. I'm good at spotting antler flashes and moose bodies slipping through the trees. Y'know, it's really hard to stay in camp when you've run out of things to do and you know there's moose to spot.

"I went just for fun and to help out, but at the end of the season Mike and Wayne handed me letters of recommendation and the assistant guide license application. They had already filled out their parts and had signed it. They told me I was good for a heck of a lot more than just cooking. So I sent the application and my money off to Occupational Licensing in Juneau, and about a month later I had my little blue license."

That first season in the field made me realize that my lifelong hunting was actually a talent, and people would pay dearly for the assistance I was capable of giving. That two guides I respected and counted as friends thought my skills were good enough to urge me to get the assistant license and later the guide license touched me. Without Hanson's and Tinker's confidence and encouragement, I doubt I would have gotten the big-game guide license. It's tough enough to be a good guide without the perceived handicap of being female to boot.

At last Wayne delivers the final load of people, gear, and shopping list items and says, "See ya in a couple days if the weather's good!"

Wayne pulls his hip boots up, shoves the plane away from shore, pushing against the float with his lean, wiry frame, then hops in. The prop spins; the engine coughs and roars to life. He taxies toward the island in the oblong lake, then turns to make a run into the wind for a quick lift off the water. He picks up speed, tips up on one float, and smoothly scoots off the lake. He circles, waggles the wings, and zooms low over the creek near the tent as he heads to base camp at Tangles.

Suddenly the men truly realize for the first time that it's just them and me all alone in the vast wilderness. That their lives, safety, well-being, and the success of the hunt depend solely on—a woman! (Some even go so far as to say, "That girl!") Expressions of doubt register in earnest when the plane disappears from sight for the last time and a deafening silence descends. No temporary reprieve because Wayne is bringing more gear. This is reality.

Is she strong enough to handle our bags? Can she drive that track rig? What if we get stuck? What if we break down? Can she spot a moose? And if she does, can she get us close to him? If we get a shot, can she skin the moose and take care of the hide and meat? For that matter, can she judge a trophy?

Wayne Hanson and his Cessna 172 at Tangle Lakes, September 1982.

It's up to me to ignore their reservations. I often feel awkward, shy, and clumsy, but I hide it. After all, I'm their fearless leader for the next week and a half. So I set about, as always, to prove their doubts are unwarranted. Later I will have the satisfaction of watching their respect unfold as they discover I do know my trade. Knowing Tinker and Hanson had enough faith in me to put me out here all by myself stiffens my "be tough" resolve. I hop up in the trailer and ask the men to toss me their gear, telling them which size bag or box I need next as the packing process begins. At first they try too hard, searching for things to hand up that aren't too heavy. Then they realize that at least my back and arms are stronger than they look. And yes, I do know how to pack the trailer so gear won't bounce around and fly out and how to tie down the tarps covering the load.

Once the trailer is loaded, we crawl into the Bombardier, our magnificent tracked all-terrain vehicle. Because the machine hauls huge loads of gear and people with minimum ground disturbance, and because it saves me from countless stints of backpacking, I affectionately call it the "Bomber-dear." It weighs four tons and can carry another two tons while pulling yet another ton in a trailer. The seven-foot-wide machine is eleven and one-half feet long, and the top of the cab is about seven feet off the ground. Although the cab of one model holds just a driver and one passenger, the cab of this particular model holds a driver who sits in the middle with a passenger on each side. In a pinch, two passengers can fit on each side. People often opt to ride standing up in the back where they can see over the top of the cab; it's a marvelous place to be to see more animals and have wider vistas to survey as we travel along.

This particular Bombardier is my favorite because its diesel engine purrs so quietly and because it has a high gear range for regular travel, plus a low range to power out of bad stucks and up steep hills—not to mention down steep hills. It's the muskeg version, which moves on two twenty-eight-inch-wide tracks and has a weight displacement ratio of slightly less than one pound per square inch on the ground. For comparison, an average person standing on two feet puts down about twelve to thirteen pounds per square inch. The Bombardier makes so little impact on the ground cover that it can be next to impossible to follow your own just-made trail back out when you've been traversing virgin territory.

As we pull away from Island Lake, I quickly explain how the men should protect themselves from the brush, whether they're riding inside or standing in the back.

"You need to watch out for slapping tree limbs when we get into a wooded area. When you ride inside, stick your elbow up—like this—instead of sticking your arm straight out." I show them with my elbow.

Wayne Hanson's Bonbardier at Island Lake camp with a load of moose and a plywood "door" to keep gear from falling out—mid 1980s.

"You can end up with a broken arm if you try to push away a branch or tree with a straight arm. And be sure to cover your face. I usually duck my head and turn as far in the opposite direction as I can, keeping my arm and elbow up. Like this." Again, I demonstrate, tucking my head into the elbow-crook of my raised arm and turning away from the imaginary limb.

"If you ride in the back, the easiest thing to do is duck below the cab. Sometimes trees will scrape right across the top of the cab, and you'll need to protect your head and face."

We cover terrain I know the machine handles easily, but that these men have never seen before. When it tilts to one side or feels like it's getting sucked into the ground I know how to compensate, but my passengers take a while to grow accustomed to the idea that nothing drastic or life-threatening is going to occur. Soon they're taken with the capabilities of the Bombardier and are full of questions.

"How steep a hill will this machine go up?" "Can it go through swamps?" "How much weight can it haul?" "What do you do when you get to a stream?" "What happens if you get stuck?"

No one remembers I'm a member of the opposite sex until one of them needs to relieve himself.

"Sharon, I've gotta take a leak," a voice fighting self-consciousness says. "Is it okay if we stop for a minute?"

"Sure. Just step behind the trailer, or go behind a tree. If you need toilet paper, it's shoved right up there in the storage box in front of your feet. I've gotta go too. I'll just head in the opposite direction. In case you ever get separated from the machine or your backpack, it's a good idea to carry a couple folded-up paper towels in your pocket. That way you're never out of toilet paper."

I show them my own folded squares of paper toweling. They give me a side-long glance and disappear. I crawl out from the driver's spot in the middle of the Bombardier, stretch, and head off to the bushes.

Experience has taught me that the best way to handle doubting hunters is to simply be myself and not force anything. Actions, not words, instill confidence. As time passes, the hunters recognize that I know my craft. They're eager to learn how to look for the large animals that blend so well into the trees, and where on the hillsides and in the valleys the moose feed, water, and sleep. I explain that a full moon can change their feeding patterns and thus the time of day we can expect to see the animals. During a full moon, they'll browse at night, making their day feeding times later in both the morning and afternoon. And brisk, cold winds will make them hole up and stay in the protection of the thick spruce forests and alder ribbons. Hard rain does the same thing.

"Where did you see that moose?" one of them will ask.

"See the gap in the mountain?" I respond. "Look straight downhill about a thousand yards and you'll see a single, real tall spruce tree with a witch's-broom[3] on top. The tree's in a big patch of short red bushes. Found it?" "Yeah," the hunter says.

"Okay, put it at eleven o'clock in your binoculars, and the bull should be at four o'clock. He's right next to a shiny, silvery-gray dead tree that's leaning at a 45-degree angle, pointing left. Behind him is a brilliant green alder bush that hasn't been frosted yet. He's popping in and out of that patch of alders as he feeds. And I think there might be a cow or a real small bull with him. Something else keeps moving up there. The bull I'm looking at is already out of velvet, but his antlers aren't white yet. He still has velvet hanging off—it looks like he's carrying long, brown squirrels—and the antlers are a deep blood-red."

"Oh, I see him," breathes the hunter.

In the early morning, as we walk from camp to our spotting point about three-quarters of a mile away, I caution the hunters to be alert.

"We've shot several moose right off the Point, first thing in the morning. They come in at night against the base of the hill to sleep and to feed. And midway down to the Point is where a game trail crosses. We might see some caribou there, and it's possible we'll see a moose."

A feeling of alert expectancy suddenly crackles in the crisp morning air.

As the days go by the men learn that moose, especially the big bulls, favor the dark fingers of tall timber that run down the hills toward glistening watering ponds. They also like the expanses of thick, green alders that cover the hills above the deep green spruce and that weave tendrils downhill through the timber. In those spruce and alder bands, freshwater springs burble up from beneath the gray-black rocks and golden moss to course downhill, joining the larger streams to fill ponds and lakes.

The hunters are curious about the moose's habits, so I explain.

"Early in the morning, just as it gets light, you'll see moose ghosting through the trees, beginning to feed. Then around ten o'clock they tend to come out on the ridges—those red knobs are a good place to check pretty regularly with your binoculars. About two in the afternoon they'll be out for a bit, and if they lie down where we can see at least an antler from here, we'll have a good chance of making a successful stalk. From about five-thirty or six until dark they're usually real active."

"What happens if we see one that we want to shoot real late in the day?" someone asks.

"Depending on how far away he is and how much he's moving, we might make a poke on 'im," I reply. "But if it's too late, we'll just watch and remember where he was the last time we saw him. If he's bedded down or was just ambling, there's a good chance he'll be near the same spot tomorrow. We'll also make some cow calls as we leave. If he's at all interested, he'll come closer."

I tell them about previous experiences with moose, both cows and bulls. Some cows—I call them the big brown belles of the boreal forest—are very inquisitive. They show no fear, and I wonder how they know they're secure, that it's the bulls we're hunting. Cow moose will pause in the full open to survey their domain. They can be so curious that they will come almost within arm's reach. Not all cows, though. Some are protecting a calf, or are part of the harem guarding the bull going into rut that has yarded them up in preparation for breeding.

Cows with calves exhibit belligerent behavior. If you get too close, their brown, calla lily-shaped ears flatten back against the head, hair bristles out everywhere, the head drops, and the body seems to grow stiff-legged and taller. That's a good time to back away. They will also give voice to their anxiety and displeasure when another animal or a human gets too near. The sound is a cross between bellow and high-pitched moan. It raises the hair on your neck and makes you trip over yourself in your hurry to retrace your steps. The sound goes on forever, as if they don't pause for breath. Maybe they needn't. Their lungs are huge.

The cows in a bull's harem aren't belligerent, but they are persistent about staying between you and the bull, running interference better than a football team. I've bumped into as many as ten cows milling around between me and the hunter, and a bull that is locatable only by the wildly flailing tree far in front of us that he's attacking with his antlers.

Near the rut, bulls exhibit incredible brute strength and dogged single-mindedness—they want their cows, at the expense of apparent good sense. One day, I watched a bull moose hook a cow under her belly, lift her, and flip her into

A cow and calf moose, Alphabet Hills, 1985.

the air to land heavily on her side. That done, he headed for his competitor—Tinker. With each stiff-legged step, the bull emitted a challenging "ulk."

Holy Hell, Tinker, I thought, *I hope Norbert shoots good.* The area was heavily wooded and thick with brushy willows, giving only two or three openings to shoot through. I, on the other hand, high on the hill with the spotting scope, could look down into the density and watch the drama unfold. The wind was still, so I could hear the moose and Tinker vocalizing and responding to each other. Norbert needed only one shot, and it's good I was high up with the scope, because the moose ran a zigzag pattern that the men couldn't see. Then he fell in a hollow so the only part visible through the scope was about ten inches of one antler. With a couple signals, I was able to direct the men to the bull. It was easy to tell when they found the moose by Norbert's astonished expletive when he saw how large it was.

When the hunters ask about bears, I tell about the night the cabin shook, especially since that's where they're staying.

It was the end of the season, and seven of us packed the cabin. Pete Buist had volunteered to sleep on the floor next to the door; I opted to be next in line since my bladder usually dictates at least one night trip. That way, I'd only disturb one person on my way out. Finishing out the floor-sleepers were my husband Michael and John Miller, a friend. Rambo, one of the hunters, was in the single bed, Tinker was in the top bunk, and John Musacchia was in the bottom. Sometime after midnight, the whole cabin jolted, hard enough to wake us up.

"Was that an earthquake?" Rambo asked, reflecting a Californian's awareness of earth tremors. A dentist in his mid-thirties, we promptly dubbed him "Rambo" because of his gung-ho attitude, full camo dress, and daily face paint.

"Nah. Didn't last long enough." The words were barely out of Tinker's mouth when the cabin jolted again.

"That ain't no earthquake, that's a bear quake," Pete muttered. "Feels like a fish on the line."

A grizzly was tugging the tenderloin section of back that we'd suspended the day before from the purlin log (main center beam) of the cabin. The tenderloin was our source of meat for the next couple of days, since Wayne had flown the rest to Tangle Lakes. A bear had already been thieving during the week when we were away from the cabin. First, it took off with the head of a twenty-pound lake trout, leaving behind the fillets. A few days later, it swiped the spruce hen that John Musacchia had shot in the morning with his bow, that time leaving behind the bird's tiny heart. Then, when we'd returned from delivering the moose to Island Lake, I rounded the corner of the cabin to find the piece of back swinging at the end of the purlin, blood dripping from the ribs where claws had raked away some meat. Fortunately, the bear had tried the spot with the toughest meat, leaving the buttery tenderloin for us humans.

Just before bed, I'd taken the precaution of removing one entire length of tenderloin, storing it safely in my big locking-lid pressure cooker. I lay on the floor, congratulating myself that at least we would have enough meat for one or two more dinners even if the bear did make off with the back.

"Pete, bang on the wall," Tinker commanded.

"No, let's yell first," said Pete. We did and the bear reacted by jerking again.

"Rambo," said Pete, "grab your arrow."

"Why?" asked Rambo.

"If you get over by the door and wait until the cabin shakes again, all you have to do is reach out and stab the bear. It's on the porch, close enough you don't need your bow," Pete responded, chuckling.

"Dammit, Pete, bang on the wall!" Tinker commanded.

"Okay, okay."

Pete banged, except he hit the plywood door, which had no latch and opened outward. As the door swung wide, the breath of seven sucked in and held as one. The bear disappeared with a "Huff" and the door banged shut.

"Jesus, Pete, I said the wall, not the door!" guffawed Tinker above the din of the laughter that our nerves released.

I also give the hunters the history of my six-quart pressure cooker. It's about my age—old for a cooking pot—and it has a history of living in hunting camps. It started out with Penny Pennington, a family friend and guide. In the fall of 1955, Penny had seen a large grizzly bear hole up; then, while flying the next spring, Penny had noticed tracks leading from the den, indicating the bear was out of hibernation. He and a hunter were approaching the den when the grizzly charged out, killing both. Local men hunted the bear down after finding Penny and his hunter; they discovered that the single shot from the hunter's rifle hadn't wounded the grizzly—it simply had a case of spring surliness and hunger from its long hibernation. I tell them that Penny's story can be found in Larry Kanuit's *Alaska Bear Tales,* a book about encounters between humans and bears. The new hunters look at me, round-eyed.

Soon a camaraderie develops and trust forms. By the second or third day we get along well and are comfortable in each other's company. And when we've successfully bagged and cleaned an animal, they laugh and talk about its immensity. The pressure's off and they're relieved. Back at camp, they allow as how they'd had serious doubts about a lady in camp. But by golly, this one's okay. In fact, they'll be back for another hunt.

"Wait 'til I get home and tell everybody a lady helped me get my moose," they say, "and if they don't believe me, I got the pictures to prove it!"

They have a new-found pride in hunting with one of Alaska's few lady guides. I smile and say thanks. Almost every group of new hunters goes through the same evolution, so it's nothing unusual for me. For them, though, it's a new and curious experience.

The single most disconcerting thing for them is when I skin the penis and testicles, then slice carefully with my knife to separate the testicles. Suddenly I hear, "What are you doing?" When I look at the men, their expressions are pained, as though I'm heading toward them with the knife. You can almost see their legs close together for protection. So I explain Alaska's proof of sex regulation. Skinning the testicles this way, one remains attached to each hind quarter. Some people leave all the male apparatus attached to one quarter, but because the hind quarters are often flown in separate loads to Tangle Lakes (the airplane can only take a certain amount of weight), we prefer one testicle per quarter. That way, any game warden at the other end will be happy.

I've found that not many men know how to deal with a woman who does the same physically demanding work they do and who stays in the same camp, sometimes in the same sleeping quarters. They always try to do the heavy things for me—lifting moose quarters, full five-gallon jugs of water—and sometimes it's easier to shake my head, grin, and let them. I wonder wryly what they think I do when they're not around. Generally, they're relieved when the hunt goes well and they've found that I'm easygoing and forthright.

The author cooking dinner at the Keg Creek cabin in 1993. Penny Pennington's pressure cooker is on the right.

Tests and Tensions

I DECIDED IN LATE SEPTEMBER, at the end of hunting season the previous fall, to step up from my assistant guide license to the registered big game guide license. Studying had consumed all my spare time since then, and now exam time was upon me. Saturday, March 18, 1989, I hopped the early evening Alaska Airlines jet bound for Anchorage where the Big Game Guide Board was meeting over the weekend and conducting guide exams on Monday and Tuesday. I purposely left early to allow a full day of uninterrupted hotel room cramming and reviewing.

As we streaked toward Mt. McKinley and Anchorage beyond, I stared at the ground thousands of feet below. Blue stubbled legions of spruce trees surrounded the snow-covered white ovals, oblongs, and sinuous swaths that had been summer's blue lakes and creeks. Other armies of distance-blued spruce marched endlessly over the far-off hills. I gazed beyond the Alaska Range, as far southeast as the horizon would let me. Not far enough into Game Management Unit 13 to see Tangle Lakes and the Alphabet Hills and Point Camp, but they were there under a blanket of snow. I wanted to wave, but didn't.

The short flight held me captive, letting my mind freewheel and offering fragmented full-color snapshots of hunting trips in the Alphabets.

There was Russell Zuryp's excitement with his first moose. He named it "John Madden Moose" after he got it home and had the head mounted. Russ suffered an illness that left him with an off-balance equilibrium and nausea the entire trip (several times I found him behind the tent, losing his just-eaten meal) but he didn't let that interfere with his enjoyment of the hunt. His partner, on the other hand, was a sourpuss who drew the chance to shoot first, shot a small moose, and then was spiteful and jealous when Russ had the good fortune to get a larger one.

And Dale Ruth, who taught me to keep twist ties, paper towels, short pieces of rope, and sundry items in my pockets. My freewheel went to freeze-frame for moment: Dale's eyes twinkled blue, his mouth curled into an impish grin. He sported a baseball cap with everything but its red bill and hatband cut away so he could wear a knit hat with it to keep his bald head warm and still shade his

31

eyes from the sun and rain. Dale, who knows the value of patience and stillness and when to build a good warm fire . . . who understands all things mechanical, along with the value of well-placed curse words.

On Dale's heels was John Musacchia, my internationally known bowhunter buddy, so patiently spending hours slowly scouring burgundy-rust hillsides step by step with his recurve in hand and me a few steps behind. His stories of early hunts in the Alphabets, other hunts in Africa. And his Italian recipes, taken straight from his posh New York restaurant to the Alphabet Hills.

Grizzly bears that walk in your footsteps so you can see their prints covering yours on your return trip an hour later. The black bear I almost threw a dishpan of dirty water on.

Fellow guides Mike Tinker, Wayne Hanson, Pete Buist, and Eric Decker. My sixty-five-year-old mom collecting a nice caribou her first day, splitting its heart in two. Babe Evans, a bundle of good cheer and the best teller of vivid hunting stories.

Fractured pictures clicked past in a slide show: pearly gray goshawks swooping to nearby treetops to scope for voles, ravens gurgling and cawing, a little ermine that finally got brave enough to sneak up to touch my boot. Brilliant fall foliage, sweet spring water, snowstorms, laughter, breakdowns, the smell of

A gray jay, or camp robber, on a shed antler at Island Lake.

onions, garlic, and fresh meat and potatoes cooking, the warmth of a wood stove after you've been soaked to the skin.

Being teased about being the only female in camp.

Frustration when hunts don't go the way you want; hunters who don't appreciate the country, are too loud, and scare all the game away. Fear on the nights grizzly bears trip on the tent ropes.

Will I remember everything I need to know when it comes time to put it on paper and talk about it?

I spent all day Sunday surrounded by notes, laws, regulations, and maps. Monday—exam day—dawned crisp and cool. I pulled open the heavy curtains and gazed out my window at the sharp-edged snow-covered mountains that nearly surround the land side of Anchorage. First shrouded in the gray of early morning, their tops began turning pink and peach as fingers of the rising sun touched them when it crept higher in the sky. My mind whirled with all the information I'd soon disgorge on paper. I feared that I would forget everything before it could spill out.

Suddenly I was blankly staring, no longer seeing the evolving colors of the mountains. I worried about how to dress so I wouldn't stick out like a sore thumb, which was going to happen anyway. I stood a good chance of being the only woman in a roomful of men bent on becoming licensed guides.

Two napping guides in 1989: rear, Mike Tinker; front, Pete Buist. They got warm in the afternoon sunshine after they dropped down out of the wind.

I'd left dresses at home because I knew they'd be wrong for this crowd, and had brought khaki-colored cotton pants, a pair of jeans, a couple of pullover sweaters and a blouse. Should I wear the khaki pants, or the jeans? What about makeup? Guides don't wear make-up (no time for it, and no mirrors either). I normally don't wear it except for dressy occasions, but today I needed some. My pale eyelashes could make my fair complexion look pasty-white, and I knew my nerves had already done that. I decided on mascara to make my eyes show up better.

Suddenly, I wished I hadn't decided to take these exams. I could be at home, getting ready for another calm day at work. No pressure. No big expectations. No stomach whim-whams.

I shook myself from my reverie and headed for the shower, thinking that afterwards a walk and a good breakfast might help settle my stomach. The walk helped, but breakfast didn't. Nerves that already ran amok got worse from the coffee's caffeine and I turned quivery.

I gave up and headed for the exam room where the examiner recognized me immediately, calling me by name. No wonder. Although I had suspected that no other females would apply to take the exam (there are only four or five women out of about four hundred guide-outfitters licensed in Alaska), I had hoped at least one might be there so I wouldn't be alone. But I turned out to be the only woman in the crowd of about twenty-five participants, and I felt small, insignificant, and extremely conspicuous all at once.

I sat up front, then thought better of it and chose a seat midway toward the back of the room. I figured I'd blend in better that way, and I could look at the others instead of feeling their eyes looking at my back.

"Ma'am, are you lost?" A deep male voice beside me registered concern. "Are you sure you're in the right room?"

"No, I know exactly where I am," I replied. "I'm here for the guide exam." The examiner chimed in, letting the man know I was supposed to be there.

The room filled slowly, and I got my share of strange looks. A couple of the men looked taken aback to see me there. But my comfort level began to go up as a few began to chat with me. It was obvious we were all anxious and jittery. One man from Kodiak said he had taken the exam last year and had failed it.

My heart sank. *Oh, no. How many others are in the same boat? Will I have to go through this again?* I already knew I would make myself take it again.

Before I left Fairbanks for the exam, one of the women in my office at my full-time job told me that she thought I just liked challenges. She knew of other ventures I had charged successfully into, so maybe she had a point. I found this challenge, leaped headlong into it, and probably wouldn't let go until I passed. In typical fashion, I hadn't had any lifelong dream or long-range plan that placed me in this room with these other potential guides. It was the newest thing in front of me, and I bit. Then I was in, hook, line, and sinker.

Once the four-hour exam was under way, all was quiet. Pencils scratched, paper rustled when pages were turned, and stomachs grumbled. I grinned. I thought of George Carlin's comedy routine about body noises always choosing quiet places to start up. The borborygmies don't play any favorites; they tell on everybody.

I raced through the exam, skimming all the questions before settling down to spew out answers. I spotted a lot that I knew, but there were a few things that I suddenly couldn't remember. Panic stirred and fluttered.

Calm down, I told myself sternly, flipping back to the first page and beginning to write.

There were sneaky things to throw a person off. One nearly caught me. We were asked to figure the Boone and Crockett score of a set of moose antlers. A good question, except for how it was laid out on the page. The numbers in the column were arranged so that sometimes the tens column was actually in the hundreds column, or in the singles column. If you added straight down the column, you came up with a wrong answer, which looked real enough to make you think it was right.

Other questions were easy. A big game tag is purchased in June. Can it be used the following January? (No. To use it in January, you'd have to purchase it in January because tags are for the calendar year: they are good from date of purchase through December 31. Harvest tickets are good for the regulatory year, which is July 1 through June 30.) How many game management units in Alaska? (Twenty-six. Many units have several subunits and most contain restricted areas of some sort, such as controlled use areas, wildlife management areas, refuges and sanctuaries, management areas, and closed use areas.) Name the most common diseases of all herbivores. (Warts and hydatid cysts.) Name additional diseases found in sheep and caribou. (Sheep get lump jaw; caribou get brucellosis.) Name five types of salmon. (King [Chinook], pink [humpy], silver [Coho], sockeye [red], and chum [dog].) Name five of the caribou herds and their approximate sizes. (Nelchina—40,000 and growing, Delta—8,000, Porcupine—150,000 and declining, Western Arctic—225,000, Macomb Plateau—700.)

If in interior Alaska the compass heading you're following is 165 degrees, what is the true heading? (The trick is to remember what latitude and longitude you're hunting in, and remember how many degrees off magnetic north you are. Alaska varies in a range of 35 degrees to 45 degrees because of its northerly and westerly position in the northern hemisphere.)

Midway through the written exam, a few chairs scraped away from the tables, and those confident souls casually turned in their papers, as if to say, "See? This is a snap." I wondered if it was really a snap, or if they might have been overly confident. I would never get to know.

It was also very easy to tell at midpoint who the ill-prepared were. They squirmed in their chairs and looked around, redfaced and distraught. Odors arose as people sweated. I'd always heard about the smell of human fear, but had never come in contact with it. I did that day, and I didn't have to be told what it was. It smelled raw and sour and sickly. Sweat from hard physical work has its own pungency, but it's a far healthier scent than fear. No wonder animals recognize the smell. This exam was deadly serious for some of these men, and it struck me that my fears were probably entirely different. For some, guiding could well be their livelihood. I was just afraid that I'd fail the exam and have to tell people about it.

What on earth am I doing here, I wondered. *I have a regular job; I could stay an assistant guide forever and be perfectly happy and never have to deal with this stress.* In the same instant I worried that I was taking it all too calmly. *Shouldn't I be more afraid?* Suddenly I realized I had detached myself from the situation and was up high in a corner of the room, observing.

I finished with about an hour to spare. It seemed, as I glanced around, that perhaps a third of the men were still in the room, sweating over the questions. *Should I have gone over everything one more time?* I worried. But I shrugged and handed the exam in anyway, knowing that test-taking studies say your first answer is usually correct.

There was nothing to do but wait until the pass/fail lists were posted later that afternoon. A few of us gathered in the hall, chattering about the questions, relieved because this part was over. The men were no longer uneasy because I was a female. We were on equal footing, bonded by shared stress. We wished each other luck and went our separate ways. To while away the time, I went to get a bite to eat. Normally I have a huge appetite, but half my sandwich went uneaten. Shopping, usually a favorite activity, wasn't very interesting either. I wandered distractedly in and out of dress shops, shoe stores, Nordstrom, J.C. Penney, B & J Surplus, music stores, and David Green, Master Furrier.

Posting time arrived at last. I ran breakneck down the hotel hall, rounded the corner leading to the bulletin board, then slowed to a walk, trying to look casual. It was apparent at a glance that about half the class had failed. I cringed. *Oh, God. Could I have failed?* I felt like peeking through my fingers to help shield the blow in case I had. I looked at the failed list first. A quick scan didn't yield my name. But the first time through the passed list, I didn't find it either, and my heart sank. Forcing myself to read slowly, I made an effort to look at every name.

I passed! Eighty out of a hundred, but I passed. Many others had similar scores. Maybe you weren't supposed to score too high on this exam. No matter.

Now it was time to worry about the oral part. I had hoped to be scheduled for one of the next day's morning sessions, but instead I drew a time slot for after lunch.

Later, back in the hotel room, I called my husband to tell him I'd made it past the first part. Michael was excited and very proud.

"All right! But don't worry so much. I know you can do it. After all, didn't I help you study? Didn't I ask you tons of questions?"

Hearing his voice settled me. I laughed, thinking about our long sessions. From January on, he had fired questions at me while I fixed dinner. Ballistics and baked beans; potatoes and gravy supplemented with game management unit boundaries.

"Yes, dear," I replied. "I'll try not to get in too big a sweat."

"Good luck tomorrow, Hon. You know what you're talking about," Michael said as we finished our conversation.

I sat back, thinking about my study helpers. Mike Tinker had also spent several hours over a couple of evenings grilling me the way the oral panel would, green eyes flashing behind his glasses as he barked out the kinds of questions he'd been asked on his exam. He leaned forward aggressively, forearms on the oak dining room table, foot tapping on the hardwood floor while his fingers drummed a similar rhythm on the tabletop.

"Describe a full curl ram," or "Name the restricted use areas in Game Management Unit 13 and what restrictions are associated with each," or "Say you have a medical emergency, and you have radio contact with aircraft. What do you do?"

I would start to answer softly. He would interrupt.

"You know how to do all this stuff. I've worked with you in the field, remember? You're better than a thousand other guides. Don't let those Guide Board guys buffalo you. All you gotta do is sound sure of yourself."

So I'd straightened my shoulders and started over, making my voice sound more positive and confident.

As I got ready for bed, I thought about Tinker's instructions. *Maybe I better practice sounding self-assured.* So I rehearsed my "confident voice" out loud, sitting up on the bed, wearing my long flannel nightshirt. I even concentrated on appropriate facial expressions. Suddenly feeling silly for gabbling out loud, I made a face at myself and scooched under the covers.

The next morning I went jogging to burn off fear- and anticipation-induced adrenalin. Thoughts flitted like chickadees through my head, winging in steep dives and banking in sharp turns. I wanted to run and scream and jump out of my skin, but sat quietly instead, quelling the urge to fidget. Studying more was impossible. At last my appointed time arrived. The licensing examiner's check-in table blocked most of the doorway, so everyone had to go past single file. The same room that yesterday had held classroom tables facing the front of the room now held four or five of those same tables. They rimmed the room, leaving the center an open, cavernous space. At each table, three guides sat on folding chairs with their backs comfortably to the wall. A lone chair, its back completely vulnerable to the open center of the room, waited on the opposite side for the hapless examinee. The silver microphone and black tape recorder on top of each table seemed enormous and intimidating. No one had said anything about the exam being recorded. The psychological disadvantage was enormous, I realized later.

I drew three old-timers. Chuck Weir was a former guide who now sells insurance, and Bud Branham and Dick Gunlogson had guided for many years. When I added up the years of experience sitting in front of me, I wilted internally. One hundred and twenty-five years of expertise! Their names had been familiar to me since childhood, particularly that of Gunlogson, who was a friend of one of the guides at Tazlina Lake, eight miles down the road from our homestead. They had good reputations, and I knew that at least one, Branham, was a master guide.

The very first question gave me pause. I was to describe the boundaries of the game management unit that I was testing to guide in, but it sounded like they thought I was testing for an adjacent game management unit.

"Uh," I said, knowing I needed to correct them, but at the same time not wishing to offend, "that sounds like Game Management Unit 14 to me. I'm supposed to be testing for Game Management Unit 13."

"Oh?" Mr. Weir checked the paperwork in front of him. "Oh, yeah. You're right." After a moment's confusion, he smiled.

"Well, let's have you describe Unit 13, then."

We were off and running. The unit boundaries were no problem, and neither were the descriptions of the special regulation areas, the seasons, ethics, or first aid. They kept asking for ways to keep flies off fresh, hanging meat, and I didn't think of one of the oldest methods of all—smoke. I had black pepper and game bags, but smoke eluded me. I felt foolish when they told me the answer they were looking for. Smoke was around before the other stuff.

And I had trouble describing how to sight in a rifle when the scope has been knocked awry. I can do it, but my trajectory description and which way to adjust got garbled, which probably didn't give me too many points.

My lack of bear guiding experience also showed, and I let myself sound hesitant. I'd had plenty of general bear experience, but not much while guiding. I had trouble discussing the positives and negatives of the spring and fall coats on a grizzly bear, and difficulty describing how to tell from a distance what a large bear looks like. I think if I had sounded more confident about any of my bear answers, I wouldn't have been grilled as thoroughly.

One of the men asked whether one's time of the month had anything to do with drawing bears, and if I'd had any problems. I paused. This was delicate territory, and I hadn't even considered preparing for such a line of questioning. In a split second, I decided that if I responded as if it was a routine question, I stood a better chance of proving to them that I could handle similar odd questions in the field with hunters.

I simply replied, "I haven't had any problems. I think it's primarily a matter of personal hygiene. I carry baby-wipes in the field, and that way cleanliness isn't a problem even if water is scarce. Leftover food is actually more of a problem in drawing bears than menstruating is."

That answer seemed to be satisfactory, and we went on to more questions on ethics and laws. "What do you do if one of your hunters insists on shooting illegal game?" "Who do you inform if you find an animal that has obviously been poached?" "Define wanton waste." Alaska, like many other states and countries, has its share of rogue guides who flagrantly disobey laws and hunting regulations. Ethical conduct is of great concern to the Guide Board and to reputable guides, and that was reflected in the number and types of questions these men asked.

That year's Guide Board was discussing whether first aid certificates should be a requirement for guides, and they wanted to know my thoughts. I thought someone responsible for others' lives, as guides regularly are, certainly should keep a current first aid card.

About an hour and a half after we began the oral exam, I found myself standing in front of the licensing board agent waiting for my final score. When all was said and done, I was given an eighty-eight for my oral responses. I had passed. My immediate reaction was an ear-to-ear grin. My cheeks felt hot, and I knew I was blushing. Even when I want to be dignified, my face does its own thing.

Just then, Dick Gunlogson called me aside. I thought he was going to offer congratulations. Instead, it was an admonishment. He cautioned me about advertising as a bear guide until I had more seasoning working for someone else. I assured him that I definitely wouldn't until I had the hunting experience under my belt and was confident that I could do a good job. I don't know if I allayed his concerns or not. I wanted him to be reassured, but I don't think he was. He turned and hurried back to the exam table to tackle the next miserable examinee.

At first I was miffed and embarrassed that he would question my integrity. His lecture made me feel puny and untrustworthy. Then the thought that he really didn't know me flashed through my mind and I remembered that he had actually been quite nice during the whole questioning process. I realized that he was most likely very concerned about ethics. My annoyance took a few moments to die away. I still wasn't happy, but I was encouraged because it appeared to me that this man took guiding seriously, and he was simply registering concern because the industry doesn't need irresponsible, unethical people working in it.

Pete Buist, one of my Fairbanks guide friends, was in Anchorage too, fulfilling his Guide Board duties by attending the weekend Guide Board meeting and doing some of the oral testing. Between giving orals he wandered over to give me a big congratulations. Talking with him immediately brought back my relief and happiness at having passed. When we finished our short conversation, I trotted down the hall toward the pay phones to call Michael, giddy grin stretching from ear to ear again.

Sleep? Not Tonight!

THE HUNTING AREA NORTH of the Gulkana River's West Fork is carpeted with brilliant rusts, burgundies, oranges, rich golds, and pale lemon yellows off-set by the dark contrast of dry brown hillsides and deep green spruce. Gur-gling creeks full of sweet, cold spring water wind their way down the mountains and through the valleys. Seventy or so miles away, the blue and white Wrangell Mountains loom over us, looking near enough to touch in spite of their distance.

Although we are in a wall tent now, we'll move into a new log cabin just as soon as we get the floor in and the roof on. In the past three days we have trundled fifty miles cross-country in our Bombardier, finding a couple of bear dens and opening up two cabins and a tent camp, readying them for the guided hunters soon to arrive. Now the chores are done, and today is ours. Mike Tinker, Dale Ruth, and I cross the canyon, hunting the high alder bushes. At this altitude you'd think the moose would need oxygen tanks.

We have a successful day. Tinker voice-calls a bull moose to within fifty yards of Dale, whose three echoing shots put it down. All three of us pitch in on the gutting, skinning, and piecing process. Curses, grunts, and groans accompany our chore, and finally the whole moose and his fifty-three-inch antlers are loaded into the Bombardier for the return trip to camp.

Backstrap with garlic and onions, fried potatoes, peas, bread, and coffee fol-lowed by my birthday cake, air-dropped from the Cessna 172 day earlier, and a swig of preventative snake medicine—a.k.a. Canadian Club whiskey—has us basking in the warm and rosy glow of a good day. The meat is hanging thirty yards from the tent on a low pole on my side of the heavy, dark-green canvas wall tent. Tomorrow's chore is to move the pole farther away and much higher. Around 9:00 in the evening we make our last calls to the "outhouse" across the trail and snuggle deep into our sleeping bags, lazily and drowsily chatting. Pleasantly tired, we are also a little silly.

A loud snort rips the night air and thundering hooves pound past on the trail a mere ten feet from the tent door. At first we're startled into wakefulness, then decide that an unsuspecting moose has frightened itself by walking up and smelling us. We drift again into slumber, only to be awakened a half hour later by whoofing, snapping sounds from the back of the tent.

Grizzly bear! The alertness inside the dark tent is palpable as the inside of my stomach curdles and tightens and my heartbeat pounds in my ears. Surely everyone else, the bear included, can hear it.

"It's only interested in the meat."

"We ought to yell."

"No, wait and see if it leaves," we whisper back and forth.

"This is ominous," Dale stage whispers, and we giggle nervously. The bear steps on the tent ropes on my side of the tent, galvanizing us into yelling at full volume. The grizzly whoofs once and is silent. Gone? We hope so. Even the little vole scurrying across the dirt floor becomes a bear noise. The late evening breeze that has picked up now scrapes branches against each other and makes fluttering leaves clearly audible. The light wind confuses the noises we have identified and become accustomed to. Ears straining, barely breathing, we listen for some sound that will tell us what the bear is up to. There it is again!

Growling and snorting, it's at the meatpole trying to tear down a piece of the moose. Flashlights on, all three of us out in our long johns, we shine the lights on the bear. The bruin's eyes glow like twin green coals. It's large all right, and no cubs in sight—a small relief. Fortunately Tinker has his short-barreled twelve-gauge shotgun, which holds six shells; it's fully loaded and in his hands. We holler once more and the bear melts into the bushes. We shine the lights all around for a few

Dale Ruth and the author, September 1983.

minutes, and see nothing except alder and willow bushes and spruce trees. All the shadows that didn't warrant a second glance earlier are suddenly unfamiliar and menacing. The hair on the back of my neck feels like it's standing up, and I shiver involuntarily. I hear shivers in Tinker's and Dale's voices.

Back in the tent, we discuss what to do next, because the grizzly will surely be back. We've noticed a distinct lack of berries in these hills—it could prove to be a bad year for bears. They're probably pretty hungry and will quickly recognize that we mean food no matter how careful we are. We decide that if the bear comes back we'll fill up the Coleman lantern with fuel and hang it up next to the meat. At least the bruin will avoid coming into the light for a while. With heavy sighs, we crawl back into our sleeping bags. No one goes back to sleep. Our breathing is shallow as we listen to the night sounds. Rustling noises from nylon-covered sleeping bags tell me I'm not the only one with a case of the quivers.

Fifteen minutes later, the grizzly is back. Out of our bags again, we rummage for the funnel, only to discover it's outside the tent. Ha. So with excellent aim, we pour the fuel directly from the can into the lantern. Amazingly, not a drop spills. The lantern is lit, and Tinker and Dale head toward the meatpole after checking to at least be sure the bear isn't visible at the perimeter of the brush surrounding the tent and meatpole. They've got the shotgun and I've got my flashlight and rifle—I'm looking everywhere at once to be sure the grizzly doesn't pop out from some unexpected quarter. The lantern is hung and we're all back in the tent.

Bill Miller bear-proofing the camp at the closeout of the 1992 season in the Brooks Range.

We wonder how it got to be 11:00 p.m. so quickly. Finally the other two doze off, and snores begin to mount. Not me—I'm wide awake with my stomach growling. That meat is on my side of the tent. With no warning the whole tent shakes and everyone starts, wide awake. The grizzly is back, and it has stepped on the tent ropes again, this time on the back rope by Dale's cot. Now it's being noisy, making a choofing sound as it exhales, blowing snot out of its nose so it can smell better. Its teeth snap together occasionally. We yell and it moves away. All three of us realize that the coffee and water we'd had with dinner wants out, but nobody is eager to go very far from the tent, much less across the trail to the outhouse. So in turn we go around the edge of the tent, flashlight in hand and another standing guard with the shotgun. The buddy system. Fine for the guys— they just stand there. Me? I have to expose my tush for the biting. I make a mental note to curtail my liquid intake earlier in the evening. This squatting exposed in the dark is for the birds.

Back in our bags for the umpteenth time, we notice it's 1:00 a.m. All three of us drift in and out of sleep. The bear circles and makes noise, whoofing and snapping its teeth until daylight. It only steps on the tent ropes twice more.

The Coleman lantern hisses as it runs out of gas around 6:00 in the morning, and I am thankful that it lasted until daybreak. We couldn't have handled a more eventful night. Deep sleep overtakes us at long last. When we awaken again, the sunlight beating on the dark green tent has made it hot inside. It's 9:30 in the morning, and we are groggy, feeling as if we've been dragged through a knothole backwards.

After a late breakfast that doubles as an early lunch, we find a new, higher location for the meatpole. It's not far enough away for my satisfaction, but we will soon move to the cabin. Hopefully, the meat won't be in such danger of being swiped by Brer Bruin. The trouble is, a lot of fresh meat sometimes over-comes a bear's better sense so it comes into camp when people are there. Bears usually stay away if there's only a little meat, say a roast or two. Then, if they come in, it often means trouble. Maybe they're stupid juveniles testing the world; maybe they're old and this is an easy meal. Or maybe they're just plain mean from an injury.

By early afternoon the pole is up and the meat moved, leaving us enough time in the day to get in some hunting. Wayne flies over to check on us and tell me happy birthday—we briefly allude to the night's events on our C.B. radio, and he chuckles. He calls any grizzly "Visitor"—he's hunted these woods for about twenty-five years now and has had many late-night bear visits, some not as friendly as others.

Funny thing. Even though we got into the birthday cake early yesterday, until Wayne flew over I hadn't remembered that today is my birthday. To celebrate, we have cake and coffee before we take off on the hunt. Air-dropped cake tastes even better than normal cake. Besides tasting good, this one is also pretty—Wayne had baked and decorated it himself. Using powdered cherry Kool-aid to color the frosting, he squished it through a plastic bag with the corner snipped off to form roses that bloomed on the chocolate icing. Then he plucked green willow leaves and tucked them under the rose petals. All my hunting season cakes came with the same thoughtfulness—much better than some expensive bakery stuff.

We take off on our afternoon hunt, but not with the same level of enthusiasm as yesterday. The hunt proves fruitless; we don't push hard because we're tired and there are still eighteen days left to the season. We look at far-off moose that we'd normally go for, but opt to wait. Besides, we have several hunters yet to arrive who are paying to hunt those moose, and lots of hard work ahead of us.

The author with her annual airdropped birthday cake in 1983, made, decorated, and delivered by Wayne Hanson.

Back at the tent before nightfall, we learn that the bear hadn't been back—all the meat was intact—and we decide it's a good thing we didn't get another moose, because that would fill up the meatpole next to the tent again and we are not looking forward to another night's entertainment. Dinner is a birthday feast of sumptuous moose stew, made by adding rice, more vegetables, stewed tomatoes, and onions to last night's few leftovers. We think only briefly about another pot of coffee before deciding against it, not wanting any late night trips outside the tent. But one celebratory dose of snakebite medicine to go with the last of the cake is in order.

About 10:00 p.m. we are in our sleeping bags, not ready to go to sleep yet, a little on edge after last night. I wonder what the night will bring.

Already I have to go to the bathroom.

Lentil & Game Stew

One 16-oz bag lentils
¼ 16-oz bag barley
1 can whole kernel corn
1 can green peas
1 can green beans
1 can diced stewed tomatoes
1 small can spicy V-8 juice
1–2 pounds stew meat (moose or caribou), cut into 1" square or smaller pieces
1 Tbsp Worcestershire sauce
2 tsp oregano
2 tsp basil
big pinch of parsley
1 chopped onion
2 cloves minced garlic
1–2 Tbsp olive oil
salt and pepper to taste
optional: ¼ cup juice from bread & butter pickle stackers, or ¼ cup lemon juice (reduces gas the next day)

Saute onion and garlic in olive oil; add meat when onion is translucent. Cook for about 5 minutes over medium-high heat, then add all remaining ingredients. Cook until lentils are soft.

Can be served as is, or over rice.

Roaming Past Midnight: A Dumb Thing To Do

W HY WERE WE OUT past midnight in the first place? One answer is simple. We had found a big bull late in the day, and the hunter had shot it. And we weren't very close to camp. It's fairly typical to find a large bull moose just as dusk is falling. Until the rut begins in earnest, the big ones generally stay out of sight except for early morning and late evening feeding. The moose, now in pieces a few miles back, had held true to form, helping to cause our present predicament. The real reason we were out in the dark was because we had made a potentially dangerous decision at the day's end. We chose to return to camp.

That morning we had headed northwest from camp while Wayne and the other hunters went in the opposite direction with the Bombardier. We probably covered ten miles on foot that day, following looping game trails. It was true September weather, sunny and crisp, the wind biting as a reminder that Mother Nature could choose snow over sunshine in a moment.

We saw several moose, but they were either too small or too far away. We'd marched through the rich fall foliage, up one side and down the other of the wooded canyon pass that joined two drainages. Then we swapped sides of the canyon again in search of the elusive better view from the other side. Finally we stopped for a late afternoon snack and to glass for one more hour from high on a grassy knoll before heading back to camp. The many grizzly bears sighted and visiting camp that year helped convince us to get back before the black of night descended.

I munched on the last of my jerky, casually sweeping the hillside across from us with my little Zeiss binoculars. Nothing had appeared down low all day, but as evening approached, a moose might meander toward the spring-fed creek that gurgled through the bottom of the valley. I had almost given up and was doing one last sweep, blindly patting the ground beside me to find the chocolate chip cookie I'd set out for dessert. A liquid brown movement caught my eye. Both hands on my binoculars now, I muttered to myself, "Cotton-picker, you big s.o.b., where did you go?"

47

"Did you find something?" Tinker had heard me.

"Yeah," I breathed, "but now I can't find him again. I only saw the body, and it's too big for a cow. Look down low; he was moving right to left. You'll see a real shiny gray dead tree with spiky limbs sticking up—I think he's left of that about a hundred yards."

"Good," he said. "All I've seen since we sat down is cows and one small bull headed in the wrong direction for where we need to go. And I hate to make Nate walk all this way for nothing."

Nathan, nicknamed "Nate," appeared to be in good shape and had hunting experience that included safaris in Africa. But he was in his mid fifties and seemed to tire easily. We had noticed a large lump under the neck of his T-shirt, the edge of it poking out occasionally. He didn't say anything about it, and we didn't ask.

"Got 'im—Jesus, he's big!" I exclaimed. "Biggest we've seen this season! Tinker, if you've got that spiky-limbed dead gray tree in the lower right corner of your glasses, he should be in the upper left."

"I see, I see," Tinker said. "Damn, you're right. He's gotta be the best so far. Leave it to the only girl around to spot the best moose." He chuckled. "Okay. Let's watch and see what he's up to. If he's just moseying and headed for the creek, we're gonna put a stalk on that bugger. Hey, Nate! Check this out!"

We both started to give Nate visual directions, but he'd been watching and listening when I explained the location to Tinker and had already spotted the bull.

"I don't know sizes like you folks do, but if you think he's big enough, I'll take him. He looks plenty big to me." Nate was ready. But while the moose was in no hurry, evening's darkness was rapidly approaching. So we scurried to re-pack our day packs, made sure extra shells were handy, and talked over the game plan. We decided on a relay that Tinker and I had developed. I'd start down the hill with Nate, to the agreed-upon spot we could see from where we stood. Tinker would keep an eye on the bull; if we could see the bull from our next lookout, we'd wave Tinker down to join us. If we couldn't see the moose, we'd move until we could, then wave Tinker down. From there, I'd wait and watch the bull while Tinker would take the hunter and go until he could see both the moose and me, then wave me down to join them. Relays work well for conditions involving thick brush and steep hills. We had both on this stalk.

Nate and I stepped over the steep edge on our knoll and walked sidehill through the grass to the edge of the alder patch that rimmed the knoll's bottom. The alders were thick—so thick we ended up crawling on hands and knees over the crinkly cornflake carpet of fallen leaves, forcing our way through the gnarly, twisted trunks. The other side of the patch gave way to scrubby black spruce interspersed with willows. Underfoot was the spongy mountain muskeg that always allows one leg to sink deeper than the other. Our next spot was perfect for seeing both the bull, which fortunately hadn't moved, and Tinker. Tinker spotted us immediately. We waved, waited to be sure he got the message, and settled in to watch our moose. By the time he reached us, the bull had switched back to the right and worked his way farther down the hill. He was in danger of disappearing from view. After a quick discussion, Tinker and Nate hustled away, working sidehill and down toward the creek. I maneuvered through scraggly spruce to an open spot a few feet down the hill. It was a smart move, because I could see the whole opposite hillside, the bull, and the creek bottom. But I might not see the two guys until after Nate shot, since our side of the hill dropped away sharply and they had disappeared almost immediately. I heard them for a couple of minutes, and then total silence fell.

I stood, alternately sweeping the opposite hillside, monitoring the moose's progress, and checking the areas below where I thought Tinker and Nate might appear. Minutes ticked slowly away. When the two men had been gone for twenty minutes, I figured they should be nearing the bottom of the hill and I might be able to see them if they went anywhere near the creek. The bull had meandered closer to the bottom of his side of the hill, which made me wonder if he'd gotten too low for the guys to see him. If either they or the moose stood in a pocket, the moose wouldn't be visible.

An uneasy feeling crept over me, telling me I was being watched. I knew the two men hadn't come back. They were hunters, which meant they wouldn't give up on the bull. Besides, we always whistle when approaching another hunter—nobody enjoys being startled—and there was no response to my two whistles. Whatever these eyes belonged to was behind me. My thoughts raced. What if it's a bear? Where are my spare shells? In my right front jeans pocket, of course. Maybe if I didn't look, I could decide this feeling was just my imagination. Should I turn around fast or slow? Fear curled icy fingers around my spine, while the back of my neck felt hot. Ever so slowly I turned, moving one foot back, slipping my rifle off my shoulder.

Two cow moose stood side by side, not ten feet away. I hadn't heard their approach. Four ears were turned toward me and four eyes stared curiously at me, moose necks stretched as far as they could. I slid my rifle sling back on my shoulder, jumped up and down, and waved both hands at the cows. Whispering "Shoo! Shoo! Git, you! Scram!" didn't work. Instead, all my quiet activity made them even more inquisitive. They stepped forward. This would not do. I had to watch the bull, try to find the men, and now worry about my backside. If these cows decided I was trouble, they could very well stomp me. I relocated, moving down the hill. The nosy moose took a couple of steps forward, closing the short distance between us. I shooed and flapped my arms, and felt immensely silly. Being quiet didn't rid me of these two, but it did help assure Nathan a shot at the magnificent creature on the other hill.

I shrugged, at a loss for what else to do to make them go away. I divided my time among looking at the bull, searching for my partners, and shooing the cows. Look across; look down; flap, flap. Eventually the cows decided I was nothing special and wandered off, straight down the hill past me. Toward the bull. A new worry—what if the cows caught the bull's attention? Or worse yet, they could bump into the hunters and spook. The direction they were headed would send them on to spook the bull.

I focused on watching the bull and on trying to find the men, wishing they would shoot and get it over with. When the shot finally did ring out, it was unexpected and I jumped. The start took my eyes and binoculars off the bull for just a second, but I quickly found him again. He had staggered forward. I caught the movement just in time to see the bull spin around and charge uphill, then swap ends and run to the left. This time he was headed down the hill. He hurtled about one hundred fifty yards beyond his starting point when his feet tangled, or the effect of the shot finally sank in, for he somersaulted. Antlers disappeared forward, followed by four long legs pawing the air as he went over. The bull tried to stand, then sank in a pile of antlers, legs, and the heavy bulk of its body.

The shot sounded like it had come from below me and to the right, which meant a cross-canyon shot of around 300 yards. The men probably had no idea where the moose had charged off to, because they were low and had to look up to see it.

Impatiently, I settled in to wait. I could see the bull, and if they couldn't find it I knew Tinker would look for me. From past experience, he knew that unless something had gone terribly awry, I would have the bull's final resting spot pin-pointed. Ten minutes or so passed before the men appeared, walking slowly. They went directly to where the moose had been when Nate shot, and began their search. Moving right, they began walking a grid pattern, looking back and forth as they inched along.

I tried mental telepathy, to no avail.

"Look at me. Look at me. I know where the moose is. Look at me! I can direct you!"

I whistled. That didn't work either. The creek was probably too noisy for me to be heard. Finally, Tinker looked through his binoculars to find me. Holding my Zeisses to my eyes with my right hand, I stuck my left arm straight out from my side, dangling my bright blue down vest. It's physically difficult to make arm movements and look through binoculars at a fixed point all at the same time. I'm amazed we can actually communicate this way. Tinker waved his hat to indicate he'd understood my signal and turned to talk with Nate. I watched the two move in the general direction of the downed moose. Twice more, they asked for a signal, and twice more I pointed left with the down vest.

As soon as they discovered the moose and had gone through a series of signals telling me to "c'mon over," I plunged straight down the hill, looking first for a few landmarks that would help me locate them. Squeezing through black spruce, slogging over soft muskeg and finding a spot along the fast, deep creek that was narrow enough to jump over, I reached them in about twenty minutes. My arrival made the skinning process go faster. They'd already taken the requisite photos and had the hide peeled away from the body in preparation for a head mount. A quick glance at our watches told us we were in danger of spending the night next to the freshly killed moose if we didn't hurry.

Nathan Johnson with a huge moose, 1983.

Nobody favored being secondary bear bait. We abandoned the painstaking caping process in favor of cutting the head off with the cape still attached and piecing up the moose so it could hang in the nearby trees to cool properly. The spruce tree branches would protect the quarters and other pieces from any rain that might fall, and we always propped extra branches against the meat for more protection. Nate began trimming the lower branches off nearby trees while Tinker and I hurriedly finished separating the body into nine pieces that would fit into the airplane. Ordinarily I could carry a front quarter without too much trouble, but this one had me staggering. It took both me and Tinker to move a hind quarter and lift it high enough to be tied off next to the tree trunk on a sawed-off branch. After hanging each quarter, we stopped for a "whoo" breather and to wipe sweat off our brows.

Darkness was descending in earnest by the time we moved the yet-to-be-caped head and all the pieces away from the gut pile and cleaned our hands and knives in the nearby creek. We had two choices. We could go to a cabin that was about an hour's walk away in the daytime, or go high on the mountain and return to our camp, about a two-hour walk during the day. Night would double the amount of walking time. At the time, returning to camp sounded like a better idea, because not only was the other cabin in the opposite direction, it had little food, no sleeping bags, and hadn't been checked out yet that season. For all we knew, a bear had broken in and made a total mess. Also, the trail into the ravine where the cabin is hidden is tough to find in broad daylight, never mind in the dark. We opted to go high on the mountain and head for home.

When we made the decision to return to camp, we recognized full well that a large alder patch lay between us and the mountain top (alders house the grizzly) and that we had to go past the meat pole loaded with an earlier moose to reach the tent. More grizzlies could await us there also. With a deep breath and a squaring of the shoulders, we began the uphill toil. Midway up the mountain we stopped to rest a moment and to eat our remaining oranges, jerky, and cookies. Full night found us traveling east toward the place where the trail dove off the edge of the mountain into the timber near camp. We stayed above the alders and below the uppermost part of the mountain. The alders, murder to get through in the daylight, were worse in the dark, and going too high on the mountain could mean breaking a leg in the dips, sheer drop-offs, and boulder piles that were everywhere. We'd have to pick our route carefully. A cold wind came up, which could send us into hypothermia if we didn't keep moving.

By 10 o'clock, in the pitch-black, we had figured out how to maintain our traveling altitude and had spaced ourselves close enough together to keep track of each other. Tinker, who knew the route and walked faster, was leading. I was in the middle, straining to see the light blue of Tinker's jeaned legs moving in front of me, then turning to hear Nate behind me. Nate was nearly impossible to see. He was a black man, which meant no light reflected from his face, and he was dressed in very dark blue. Tinker hollered back to me when he stumbled into a nasty rock pile, and I relayed the info farther back to Nate. That way, at least two of us avoided most of the pitfalls. When I heard that Nate had wandered up or down the hill, I'd redirect him.

"I'm over here, Nathan, go to your left." Or, "Go to your right." When I could no longer see Tinker's legs, I'd stop and listen for footsteps crunching and stumbling both in front and in back of me. When Tinker or Nathan couldn't be seen or heard, I'd yell, "Tinker, wait up. You're getting too far ahead of us." I would wait until Nate caught up with me; then the two of us joined Tinker and we set off again on our stumbling march.

We stopped to rest and guzzle water two or three times during the four-hour walk, grateful for the break, shivering as the wind chilled us. Our legs were wobbly from walking unevenly and uncertainly in the darkness, our eyes burning from straining to see.

We were high enough on the mountain to see Island Lake in the valley below, which told us we hadn't gone too far. It also told us we needed to drop down toward the timber, or we would be in danger of continuing around the top of the mountain and having to spend the night out in the wind. I hadn't said anything to the other two, but I knew hypothermia had become a more real danger than it had been earlier. Our bodies were out of fuel from the hard walk, which meant we wouldn't warm very easily if we had to spend the night out. We were sweaty from exertion and our clothes were damp. Every time we stopped, I shivered. The mountain breeze chilled us all.

Finally, Tinker and I agreed that we should be in just about the right area to begin looking for the Bombardier trail off the top of the mountain. I hauled out my very dim flashlight, cursing myself for not remembering to change the batteries that morning. It only took a few minutes to find the faint Bombardier track marks leading toward the tent. We cheered tiredly, now that the pressure of wondering if we would make it back had dropped away. Midway through our midnight march, the three of us had realized we'd made a foolish decision back at the moose when we chose to go anywhere. We should have either headed the other direction to the cabin, or gone a few hundred yards away and holed up under a tree until dawn. We could have roasted moose on a stick over the fire we'd have had to keep burning all night. Now, only one more hurdle remained, and that was to reach the tent and the cabin with no grizzly bear encounters.

"Time to be noisy," Tinker announced. "I don't want to surprise any bears at the meat pole. Sharon, keep your flashlight out, and you and I put a shell in the chamber."

Reaching in my jeans pocket, I pulled out the shell that was my fifth shot. Feeling my way, I stuck it in the chamber of my 30.06. Click, click.

Both our rifles on safety, flashlight in my shirt pocket, and all three of us with dry mouths, we headed down into the closeness of the timber. It was 1:00 a.m. The trail we felt our way along wound through tall, dark spruce trees toward the tent. And toward the meat hanging on the meat poles directly between us and the tent. From the many nocturnal grizzly bear visits during the first half of the hunting season (they had been doing a nightly tap dance on our tent ropes), we fully expected to encounter one of our now too-familiar bruins. A perfect place for us to find him, or him to find us, would be upwind from the meat—exactly where we were walking. Unfortunately, we had no other route. In the pitch-blackness of the night, the trail was our only hope of reaching camp.

Small talk, which accidentally burbles out when you're supposed to be quietly hunting, was difficult to come by. Especially loud small talk. A strained conversation would start, then peter out. We talked about grabbing the sleeping bags, extra flashlight batteries, some food, and the Coleman lantern out of the tent so we could spend the night in the cabin. We needed to rest our frayed nerves and bodies.

All was quiet, then Nate asked, "How do you manage to think of what to talk about? All I can think of is bears." "I don't know," I replied. "My mind is blank. Maybe we should sing."

"Okay. You think of something," Tinker said.

"Oh, thanks," I replied sarcastically, "leave it to me to be the entertainment." I thought, then blurted out a silly ditty.

> *Oh, I wish I were a little keg of beer!*
> *Oh, I wish I were a little keg of beer!*
> *I'd go downey with a slurpey,*
> *And I'd come-ey up with a burpey!*
> *Oh, I wish I were a little keg of beer!*

I sang, to Tinker and Nate's amusement. Their too-loud laughter sounded as nervous as I felt. I sang at what felt like the top of my lungs, but my voice sounded like it came out thin and reedy. To my ears, my voice sounded infinitesimally small, a feeble gesture against the dark and grizzlies. I thought of Penny Pennington, and of Cappy Caposella, another guide who died after a grizzly mauling. His friend saw the whole thing, including the bear with Cappy's head in its mouth, swinging him like a rag doll. I wanted to get to the tent, and then farther down the hill to the new log cabin with no such encounters.

"Is there more?" they asked.

"Yeah," I said. And I started into another verse, as off-key as before.

> *Oh, I wish I were a George Washington!*
> *Oh, I wish I were a George Washington!*
> *I would cross the Delaware without any underwear!*

Oh, I wish I were a George Washington!

Nate laughed. "Where did you learn that?" he asked.

"With her, you never know." I could almost hear Tinker shaking his head. "She comes up with some of the most off-the-wall stuff. Are there any more verses?"

"Yup," I replied. "You wanna hear 'em?" They did. They thought I was doing an excellent job of keeping the bears away.

Oh, I wish I were a little sparrow!
Oh, I wish I were a little sparrow!
I'd sittey on the steeple,
and I'd spittey on all the people!
Oh, I wish I were a little sparrow!

Oh, I wish I were a little bar of soap!
Oh, I wish I were a little bar of soap!
I would slippey and slidey over everybody's hidey,
Oh, I wish I were a little bar of soap!

I finished the last verse and fell silent. Then we sang "She'll be Coming Round the Mountain," and were quiet again. Now we were only about a quarter mile from the tent, not a good place to be quiet. We all jabbered at once, loudly. Nate mentioned the bottle of Scotch he'd brought for a special occasion. Shooting the moose today, completing our midnight march, and reaching the cabin tonight without any bear frights was just that occasion.

Suddenly we were at the meat pole. It was dark enough that I'd missed the big rock beside the trail that told me where we were. There had been no bears! We checked the meat, and found that again no bears had visited.

Quickly untying the tent flaps, I reached for my dying flashlight while Tinker struck a match. I grabbed the Coleman lantern from inside the tent, and held the flashlight while Tinker lit the lantern. Nate grabbed his Scotch, Tinker snatched his frame backpack and stuffed our sleeping bags in it, and I corralled coffee cups, plates, eating utensils, coffee grounds, onions, spices, and some cans of God-knows-what. I knew we didn't have much for dinner, since I'd sent all the meat with the crew in the Bombardier. If I'd been alert earlier, I would have grabbed a bit of fresh moose before we took off for camp, but our minds had been on one thing. Finish and get out of there.

We staggered into the cabin. Nate parceled out three healthy shots of scotch. One sip prompted me to ask, "What is this?" It was the smoothest I'd ever tasted.

"Glenlivit," Nate replied. "For hunting trips, I get nothing but the best. It took me a long time to decide between Glenlivit and Glenfiddich, and I think I picked the right one. Is there an extra onion I could have?"

"An extra onion?" Tinker sounded puzzled. "Sharon's making dinner."

"I know," Nate said. "But my wife won't ever allow me to eat raw onions around her, and I love 'em. Would it be okay if I ate one here? Will either of you mind?"

I giggled, feeling flushed and foolish. The smooth Scotch on an empty stomach took effect fast.

"Sure, it's okay," Tinker said. It's just—nobody's ever asked that before."

The soup was ready in a few minutes, but was a bit thin. I'd hoped the cans that I'd grabbed from the tent would be vegetables, but they turned out to be mostly peaches and pears instead. It didn't matter. The Scotch had warmed us and made us silly, and the canned fruit turned into dessert.

We decided we'd sleep in the next day, eat a good breakfast, and then Tinker and I would walk back over to the moose while Nate rested. We had to finish removing the cape from the head, hang the neck and back, and bring some meat and the cape back with us. I planned to rescue the two strips of tenderloin from the inside of the lower back. No sense letting the gray jays we call camp robbers peck away the good stuff. Besides, we wanted to see if a bear had found the meat.

The lantern was out, and we were cozily in our sleeping bags discussing Nate's moose and treasuring the four solid walls surrounding us. Those walls were especially precious that night, as we agreed how fortunate we were to be inside instead of bumbling around in the cold, black night. Without saying so, we all recognized that we'd erred when we decided to return to camp.

We hadn't taken the time to measure the antlers, and our guesses ranged from fifty-seven inches to sixty inches. I knew it was a heavy rack, because my hand hadn't reached all the way around the beam where it attached to the head.

That reminded me.

"Oh, Nathan. I forgot. Congratulations. That was a helluva shot. How far do you guys think it was?"

Tinker said he estimated it at roughly 350 yards.

Then the talk turned to our long walk back. Nate was astonished that we'd managed to get back and find our trail off the mountain. He and Tinker began telling stories, bears topping the list. I listened, eyelids growing heavier and heavier, their voices drifting away to a far-off murmur.

The last thing I heard was Nate singing to himself, "Oh, I wish I were a little bar of soap!"

Moose Studies: Guides Help Department of Fish and Game

CAMP ROBBERS ALREADY CHATTERED and fussed overhead as I braced myself, reached over the moose, and took a firm grip on the edge of the saw cut that was opening the brisket, or breastbone. I pulled up firmly and evenly, trying not to lose my balance and accidently put more weight on the part I was trying to lift. Mike Tinker continued his steady sawing, opening more and more of the chest cavity.

"Hey, Tinker," I blurted. "We gotta get a blood sample for Zarnke!"

I had suddenly remembered the blood samples we were supposed to collect for Randy Zarnke, a biologist in the Alaska Department of Fish and Game (ADF&G), Division of Wildlife Conservation in Fairbanks.

We stopped butchering. I snatched a plastic Ziploc bag from its resting place beside our packs amid the lowbush cranberry and blackberry bushes. It held the necessary vials, syringes, and last but not least, the instructions. Fortunately, a large quantity of blood was still pooled inside the moose's rib cage, so we busied ourselves filling the syringe, carefully squirting the blood into the appropriate containers, and leaning them up against the base of a nearby spruce tree to settle. The instructions said to "disturb the tubes as little as possible; do not purposely shake," and we did our best to comply. The idea was to keep the vials as still as possible (a neat trick when your trip back to camp is up hill and down dale over rough terrain, whether on foot or in the Bombardier). Another vital step is to keep the tubes from freezing. Or from sitting in a deep pocket of your backpack in the warm sun for a couple of days. Those are the times your nose leads you to the discovery that you've forgotten to finish the sampling task. By the next day, ideally, the blood separates into two parts, one a thick red clot on the bottom and the other a yellowish liquid serum on top. We were to draw off the serum with a plastic pipette and squirt it into the small screw-cap vials provided in the blood sample kit. The final step involved recording vital statistics, including the collector's name, date of collection, sex and age of the animal, and the geographical location in which the animal was harvested. If we notice any other

57

unusual characteristics, such as hydatid or tapeworm cysts, legworms or tumors, we try to remember to record that information too, even though the instructions don't ask for it.

Intent on collecting the samples and on keeping them as clean as possible, we momentarily failed to notice our hunters' quizzical expressions as they watched us make a temporary switch from skinners and butchers to preoccupied (mad?) scientists. Before the second vial was filled, their curiosity won out. They bombarded us with questions, mostly relating to what earthly reason we could have for collecting blood out in the bush and why we were going to so much trouble. We explained our assistance to Fish and Game and Randy Zarnke's work.

He studies the serum from moose and other animals to determine their general health as well as whether there are infectious diseases, viruses, antibodies, and parasites. This information, collected from animals harvested during hunting season as well as those that are purposely captured live, sampled, and released, helps discover how or if any of these factors contribute to mortality rates. For the biologists, the blood we collect from this and other moose provides a wealth of information and at no cost to them.

For our part, once we knew the moose were being studied, our interest was piqued. We joked that if the moose in our area proved to be particularly disease-free and otherwise healthy, perhaps we could market hunts for "ADF&G Approved" game! Kind of like the Good Housekeeping Seal of Approval.

The sera tests and their results are quite important to both biologists and guides. Guides and hunters benefit by knowing whether the game in the area they hunt is healthy. Most guides keep a keen eye on the game populations in the areas they work, managing the resource so the population doesn't become depleted. Guides conduct hunts in different parts of an area from year to year so one location doesn't suffer from overuse. If disease is killing the animals, it's also wise to avoid hunting in the area, so human consumption and disease don't combine to lower the animal population to a point where it can't recover.

Knowing what the disease is can be helpful in other ways—some diseases pose a health danger to humans, to dogs, or to both. In general, diseases in moose aren't harmful to humans or other animals, but other animal diseases can be. For instance, parvo virus and distemper are detrimental to dogs, and rabies and tularemia are harmful to both dogs and humans. Some diseases could decimate an entire animal population.

Alaska's biologists began this study around the time of statehood. In 1959 or 1960, the initial work started with sampling the Delta bison herd to find out if it might be suffering from brucellosis, as the Yellowstone National Park bison were (results showed the Delta bison to be free of the disease). Brucellosis is a bacterial disease in cattle and people that causes fever, as well as joint pain similar to arthritis. Knowing the baseline data in the Delta bison herd area would help biologists keep tabs on the health of the animals. Other animals were added to the study over time. Randy took over the program around 1979 and was instrumental in expanding the focus on both the host and the disease side. The program has grown to include diseases in nearly all wildlife populations. Currently, the animals studied in Alaska include moose; caribou; Dall sheep; bison; deer; elk; red and arctic fox; wolves; mountain goat; musk ox; the raven; snowshoe hare; lynx; wolverine; all seals; sea lions; walrus; sea otter; grizzly, black, and polar bear; and miscellaneous smaller animals.

According to Randy, the disease survey's purpose can be described in two different ways, depending upon one's persuasion. It monitors the overall health status, or it monitors the disease status of the wildlife in the state.

Randy Zarnke, Alaska Department of Fish and Game biologist, with a caribou at Tangle Lakes, about 1984.

Discovery of disease often leads to research that will provide more knowledge about the disease or help to devise a way to cure or counteract it. For instance, a vaccine that can be orally ingested in bait could be developed to counteract a disease. The vaccine would be useful in a bait in the wilderness or in a more controlled situation such as in zoo-bound animals' food.

Our sampling assistance began in 1985 and continues each fall during moose hunting season. The approximately ten thousand moose sera sampled statewide over the last twenty or so years have proven the moose to be quite healthy and mostly disease-free. The study results provide insight into the overall health and the incidence of diseases, viruses, and antibodies in the animals sampled. They will also translate into further research to control the diseases, to learn how to combat the diseases if they become epidemic, and to learn more about how animals react or adapt to new diseases or new strains of disease.

As we take blood samples from the animals we're dressing for our hunters, I wonder what the serum will reveal about that particular critter and take extra pains to ensure that the sampling gets done right. Our part in the whole process may be small, but it takes all the small parts to fill in the empty spaces in the animal health and disease puzzle.

A Macho Alaska Wilderness Experience

MIKE TINKER, MY THEN-BOYFRIEND Michael Everette, and I began the morning at Point Camp, closing it up from the 1985 hunting season before heading for the Keg Creek cabin to pick up Don Wanie and Hank Masters, drop-off hunters from Juneau. We were in high spirits. The season had been fun, and we were heading out right on schedule. Snow from two days before hadn't melted at the highest elevations, but most of our trail would be out of the snow. Autumn's colors were in full blaze, brightened by the crisp sun. Because most of the alders and willows had dropped their brown and yellow leaves into a blanket on the ground, we were treated to the deep burgundy and rust of the frosted dwarf birch against that golden backdrop. The deep olive-colored spruce trees stood proudly in muted contrast to the brilliance of the other colors.

We arrived at Keg in time for dinner. Don had chicken out, a wonderful change from a twenty-day diet of moose. Don and Hank were perfectly happy when I offered to fry it up for the five of us—they'd had enough of their own cooking.

Don and Hank were nearly ready to go; Wayne was scheduled to fly them out of Caribou Lake early that afternoon so the men could easily make their ferry reservations at Haines. The lake was about two hours of Bombardier time away.

"Hey, we heard you coming! Coffee's on," said Don. "We're all packed up and ready to go. All we have to do tomorrow is take the chimney out and empty the ashes out of the stove. The plywood is on the back window, but I left the door one off so we still get natural light." Don's face, haloed by short curly brown hair, carried his usual happy grin as he met us on the trail just outside the cabin.

"Great, let's have a cup and then get the moose. We need to be sure we get you to Caribou in plenty of time for Wayne to make lots of trips. I hear you got two moose," replied Tinker.

"Yeah. They're real easy to find, and I think they're near the trail we have to take out of here. Hey, Hank, come meet these guys," Don said over his dark red wool-jacketed shoulder toward the cabin, then turned back to us.

61

A tall, lanky man with graying hair and a blue coat stooped to avoid hitting his head as he stepped out the cabin door. He frowned at the sky, which was beginning to turn gray and heavy with clouds, as he came out.

"Hi, Hank. Good to meet you," I said as Don introduced him to each of us. "How was your trip? Did you have fun?"

"I sure did. C'mon in and get some coffee."

"Okay," I replied. "Let's use the cups from the cook box on the machine so you don't have to unpack yours."

"We saw lots of animals," Hank continued. "And this is sure big country. It seems like a person could get lost out here and never be found. All these hills look the same."

"Yeah, I know," I said thoughtfully. "That's why I always pick a spot on the horizon to mark where I'm at. Of course, that's no help if you get fogged in. Then, you hope you have a compass and you thought to get a heading. Or else, stay put until the fog lifts. Big spruce trees come in handy then."

By the time we got up in the morning, the weather had turned, almost viciously. Snow was coming down like salt out of an inverted shaker with big holes, covering the vivid colors I had hoped to see on the way out. Tinker, Michael, and I decided we were probably in an isolated storm pocket and would be out of the nasty stuff after a few hours. We believed in positive thinking.

Tinker, Don, and Mike loaded all the gear while Hank and I finished closing up the cabin; the three of them got done just as Hank and I did. Just then, we heard Wayne's airplane. I frowned, and Tinker and I exchanged a puzzled glance. He ran for the cab of the Bombardier, turned on the key, and grabbed the hand-held transmitter of our CB radio.

"Hey Scout, do you read me?" Tinker asked.

"Yeah," Wayne crackled. "I'm heading to Willow while I can. The lake at Tangles is freezing over, and I can't land at Caribou Lake—too much ice on the edges. It's beginning to storm pretty good. Don and Hank will have to ride out to the road with you."

"Okay. We'll get the tent and stove and gear from Caribou," said Tinker.

Sometimes, Wayne would haul the smaller tent camps out to Tangles in the airplane, especially if we had several moose to haul and many miles to cover. Not this time.

"Zarnke's got a moose for you to haul," Wayne continued as he circled above. "It's off to the right of the trail about a mile before Trapper. You'll see it easy if you go one ridge over."

"We'll get it. Take care of yourself, old man," Tinker said as he signed off. Wayne planned to drive back to Tangle Lakes that afternoon to meet us and get the Bombardier.

Wayne's white airplane disappeared into the swirl of cloudy, blowing snow and left our hearing range almost as quickly as he lifted above the high pass hidden by the storm.

Our high spirits shifted into determined hustle as we reorganized, knowing we had a long haul ahead of us. Not getting rid of two passengers and their moose at Caribou, and no one being able to ride in the back because of both the snowstorm and the unanticipated gear meant we had to pack extra carefully.

We were also faced with having to turn a comfortable two-day trip into a one-day charge for the road so the Juneauites could get to Haines to keep their ferry reservations. Getting from Tangle Lakes to Haines, about a 650-mile drive, is no small feat in good conditions. If the weather turns snotty, as it often does toward the end of September, the trip can be torture.

I hope we don't get stuck, I thought as we clambered into the Bombardier for the trip to Caribou Lake. There is no trail between Keg and Caribou, so you're always wandering along in new territory. Plus, there is one creek that is purely devilish to cross.

With a Bombardier, you need to look for a lot of things at once: a stream crossing with a hard bottom or else thick, strong willows to hold the machine up, a bank on the opposite side that the machine can climb, no sheer bank dropoffs where you need to plunge into the stream, and no deep channels anywhere in your way across.

This particular creek meanders through a small draw that has all sorts of bad crossings: steep sides, squishy creek bottom where it does widen out, and some spots so steep you'd swear that if you tried to cross (and we wouldn't!) the trailer would stand on its tongue going down one side while the Bombardier tried to go up the opposite side. It would be a "V" shaped jackknife job that no trucker could handle, that's for sure.

Luck stayed with us, though, and after several stops to get out and walk along to investigate, we found a decent crossing. We reached Caribou Lake with no mishaps.

The wind, however, was beginning to howl in earnest. My cold fingers fumbled over packing the cook pots, Coleman stove, lantern, and small quantity of food. I tried to hurry while the men untied the ropes guying the wall tent with their ever-stiffening fingers. As soon as the green tent was untied, Tinker and I banged the ice off the outside walls from the inside with our fists and then pulled out the spruce poles that held the tent up. Quickly folding the ends in and the sides in thirds, we thirded it again and roughly stuffed it into its burlap sack.

Thoroughly chilled, we hopped back into the machine and trundled toward Trapper. Away from the lake, the wind calmed a little. Soon we were through the pass between Caribou and Trapper. We began to look for the flagging that Randy Zarnke had placed on the trail to show where to turn off for his moose. Fifteen minutes after finding the flagging and leaving the trail, we came to the pieced-up moose. Some pieces hung from sawed-off tree branches and others were carefully laid out on the tree branches that Randy and his partner had cut. We put his moose in the back of the machine where people usually stand, since we were cramped for space and it was too cold and miserable for people to ride out in the weather.

At Trapper Cabin, we corralled up the food and cooking utensils that needed to go with us and stuffed them in a designated box. We nailed the door shut and covered the window with plywood so a grizzly bear wouldn't swat the glass out. Back in the Bombardier, shivering until each other's body heat took the chill off, we settled in as Tinker shifted into second gear. All five of us—Don, Hank, Tinker, Michael, and I—were crammed into the front seat of the Bombardier, which usually holds three, held in by makeshift plywood "doors," grayed with age. Those old pieces of plywood blocked the wind and snow from only the lower half of our bodies. The doors had to be wedged in after everyone was seated—sometimes the two people on that side of the machine would have to shift positions enough so the door would go in, and then reposition to semi-comfort. Blue plastic tarps tucked in and tied at the top of the door frame semi-protected our top halves.

The Bombardier growled up the steep hill, one of the many that seem to be a trademark of the places that Wayne and his brother Mel chose to put a camp, long before Tinker started working for Wayne.

After making the long, slow climb out of Trapper, Tinker decided to take a more direct route than the meandering small trail we usually used. Going cross-country would take us to one of the area's main trails near the Middle Fork of the Gulkana River more quickly than following the trail.

"Michael, take a look. This thing is steering awful hard," Tinker said about an hour later, as he stopped our crawling uphill climb on our new cross-country route. Michael removed the plywood door and half stepped, half fell out of the Bombardier's cab. I poked my head out to watch, squinting into the stinging, wind-blown snow. Michael plodded through the deepening snow toward the back of the machine, then stopped in surprised midstep. He turned around, eyes wide. I expected to hear that a tree was caught in the tracks, or the trailer was dragging a big stick.

"We lost the wheel on the trailer!" Michael blurted in astonishment.

Lost the wheel! I drooped. We had two moose, two tent camps, and gear from three cabins in the trailer. The rear of the Bombardier held one moose and all our personal gear. We were supposed to turn a two-day comfortable trip out into a hard-charging one-day trip to the road. Now what?

"What'd he say?" Tinker asked.

"The wheel came off the trailer," I replied, eyebrows raised.

"Whaaat?!" Evidently, Tinker hadn't expected to hear that either.

Everyone got out of the Bombardier and milled around in confusion. We bumped into each other and babbled at the same time—I felt like I was in a Keystone Cops movie.

It didn't take long for part of a plan to evolve: find the wheel and unload the trailer. Tinker and Michael back-tracked on foot to find the wheel. When they located it not far down the hill, they also discovered that the axle had snapped. It was obvious that the trailer had been rolling on borrowed time, as the majority of the crack was very dark. Time had allowed it to oxidize. Only about an inch of the three-inch thick square army trailer axle showed the shiny newness of a fresh break. It had snapped under the stress of bouncing over a downed tree.

It took all four men to roll the wheel up the hill. While they cursed as they alternately rolled and pushed the recalcitrant wheel, I spread two tarps on the ground—one for gear and the other for meat. We emptied the trailer, then covered the piles with more tarps to keep the snow off. Then it took all four men to load the heavy, awkward wheel into the trailer.

The broken axle put a kink in our plan to speed toward the road so Don and Hank could meet their tight schedule.

"I think we can make the road late tonight, if we can find the trail," Tinker said to Don and Hank. "It means we'll have to drive a lot of the way in the dark. But that way you can get a night's sleep before you have to drive."

"Yeah. We ought to try for the road," said Don after a brief discussion. We unloaded Randy Zarnke's moose from the Bombardier and replaced it with Don and Hank's two moose. We also loaded Don and Hank's gear in the Bombardier, along with a tent camp, food, and Tinker's, Michael's, and my sleeping bags. Somebody would have to come back for everything left behind.

We put the wheel in the trailer, since we needed to get it to the road. Tinker and Michael cut a spruce tree long enough to form a travois, or a skid, to hold up the wheel-less side of the trailer. With a little finagling, the tree was tied and chained firmly in place.

As soon as the five of us wedged ourselves back in the Bombardier with the plywood doors, we moved off slowly. We purposely left the tarps off so we could keep a watchful eye on the trailer's progress. We weren't sure how well it would negotiate the dips, tussocks, and trees we had to wallow through. Our confidence grew; the trailer seemed fairly stable, so we put the tarps back in place to keep what warmth we could inside the machine.

Soon we were traveling in a whiteout. Besides the heavy snow falling and the cold wind swirling it all about, fog had settled in. About every ten or fifteen minutes, Tinker would be forced to stop because he couldn't see for the snow plastered against the windshield. Either Michael or Hank would get out, clean off the heavy snow, and then wedge themselves back in.

Besides wretchedly awful weather, we had to contend with the fact that we couldn't back up with the tree under the trailer. Where the wheels simply rolled, the tree would dig in. We couldn't allow ourselves to come up to any sheer dropoffs or bad creek crossings. We had to have room to turn the Bombardier before plopping into a bad situation. No one except Tinker and I had spent much time in a Bombardier before this trip, so we had our eyes glued to what little ground we could see in front of us. Fortunately, Michael had experience outdoors and was good at seeing terrain, so his eyes helped.

Hank was worried because we had no trail. He tried to use his compass inside the Bombardier until he realized the compass wouldn't read correctly inside that big lump of metal. At nearly every stop, he would haul out the compass and try to decide what direction we were going, and if we should try some other direction. We didn't stop for lunch, munching instead on trail food as we went along.

Tinker, who can read this country better than most people can decipher road maps, would recognize some blurred landmark on the horizon through the heavily falling snow every now and then. The trouble was, though, the only "horizon" we had was about twenty yards out.

Using a log as a travois for the Bombardier trailer. This was when the trailer had a flat tire in 1997.

In spite of the fear that he and Hank might miss their ferry reservations, Don was particularly cheerful. Every now and then, as the day wore on, he would pipe up, "This is really a macho Alaska wilderness experience. I wouldn't miss this for the world!"

About 7:30 in the evening, the weather cleared and the fog lifted, leaving a bluish-pink dusk as the sun dipped down for the night. We were able to move a little faster, and every now and then thought we saw the trail we needed to find so we could run into the night—until we reached the Denali Highway—but it proved to be elusive.

Finally, we came to an open field that had one lone, very full spruce tree at one end.

"Tinker, I think the trail has to be right over there," I said as we neared the tree. "I could swear I see it over near that timber."

Tinker started to continue on, but we all had noticed that the lone spruce was at the edge of a perfectly flat dried out pond bottom. What better place to pull the Bombardier alongside, leaving enough room to tie one end of the tent to the machine and the other to the tree? So he circled back around.

We whacked branches off the one side of the tree to make room for the tent to nudge up against it. Those branches went on the ground inside the tent, and made the most comfortable bed any of us had ever slept on. While the men scrounged wood for a campfire, I hauled out the Coleman stove and heated water for something hot to drink. As soon as the fire was roaring, we began to rotisserie ourselves to thoroughly warm all sides. We also dried gloves, hats, jackets, and mittens. Michael had my good Red Hot brand wool insulated mittens on the end of a stick to dry them, and burned a hole right through the end of one. Poor man. To this day, I've not let him live that mishap down. When I find some article of clothing that keeps me warm, I jealously guard it. He didn't know that then.

Hot chocolate was the drink of choice. I don't remember what dinner was, but as soon as it was in us, we crawled in our sleeping bags and were asleep in an instant.

Dawn came early, it seemed. None of us were eager to crawl out of our warm cocoons, but we knew we needed to get moving, because it was 7:00 a.m. and the time for Don and Hank to reach Haines had dwindled beyond comfort. As we popped out the tent door one by one, we discovered the storm had, indeed, departed. The morning sky was the steel blue that follows an early autumn snow storm. White hills and snow-shrouded brush softened the effect. Tree trunks look like pencilled sticks. Two browsing moose were a stark contrast against the sharp white hillside.

Campfire roaring once more, we all kept warm as I made coffee and heated water for our instant oatmeal and hot chocolate.

"What did I say?" Don announced gleefully. "A true macho Alaska wilderness experience! Man, this is the best place to have one."

I grinned at him. His good cheer helped ease the tension I felt about getting him and Hank to the road late.

"And what a crew to experience it with. Man, it doesn't get any better than this. I don't care if I ever get back to work."

Don was enjoying himself, and Hank seemed less tense than the day before. Perhaps the storm being gone had helped relax them, as had a good night's sleep. Perhaps also they had accepted the idea that they might not get to Haines on time and were no longer as worried about time schedules.

We stuffed our sleeping bags into their sacks so Tinker and Michael could take the tent down. A quick inspection of the trailer travois proved that it was working successfully.

Soon we were loaded and rolling, this time without the tarps in the doors. It felt good to face sunshine instead of stinging wind and snow.

"Well, I betcha the trail is right over there," I said to no one in particular.

Above: The Macho Alaska Wilderness Experience camping spot. Note the wheel in the trailer and the log that forms the travois.

"Probably," Tinker replied, as he set a course angling toward the timber.

My mind had wandered off into the day-dreamy, introverted state that drowsiness and a monotonous noise (like the sound of the Bombardier engine running) can trigger, when I realized we had just crossed a wide white swath that looked a heck of a lot like the trail we needed.

"Hey, Tinker," I blurted, jarred into awareness, "I think we just crossed the trail!"

He stopped. We had gone only about a hundred yards from our campsite. With a big grin, he swung the Bombardier to the right and guided the machine onto the sparkling white ribbon that wound toward the Denali Highway.

"Well, gang, we'll hit the road in no time!" He put the machine in third gear for fast trail running, thankfully smoothed by several inches of cushioning snow.

Soon we discovered we were following the footsteps of a large lone grizzly bear. The bear tracks wandered from side to side of the trail, occasionally leaving for a few hundred feet, then ambled along again. Evidently this trail provided prime back scratching opportunities, because the bear would periodically walk up to a spruce tree—partially denuded on the trail side—turn around and rub back and forth, up and down against the tree. It left plenty of hair as testimony to either a very itchy back or a tree that felt pretty good. We stayed with the bear for about four hours, until we were about four miles from the Denali Highway. Then the grizzly left the trail and we never crossed tracks again. Perhaps it knew it was reaching an area more populated by humans.

When we arrived at the road, we discovered that Wayne must not have arrived from Willow, because he and the truck to haul the Bombardier weren't there to meet us. With an undercurrent of worry, Tinker and I quickly opted to walk the two and one-half miles to Tangles to bring two vehicles back, while Michael helped Don and Hank unpack their gear and moose from the Bombardier. As soon as we brought their pickup, they would load up and zip down the road to Paxson where there was a phone so they could let the Alaska Marine Highway System know of their tight time schedule—and the dilemma that had caused it. With tourist season over, the ferry system was a little more prone to adjust their schedule to meet local passengers' needs.

We had walked only about half a mile when a road crew pickup with Roger Butler, the Department of Transportation and Public Facilities' maintenance foreman from Paxson, crested the hill and coasted toward us. Tinker and I both knew the man, who gave us a ride in the back of the pickup—a bit cold, but much faster than walking!

When we got back to the Bombardier with the pickups, the men had completely unloaded the machine. Don and Hank filled the camper shell with their moose and gear, said good-bye, and about two in the afternoon, headed east toward Paxson and the long road home. Their ferry reservations in Haines were for the 6:00 the next morning. They had sixteen hours to drive 650 miles.

Since Wayne wasn't back, we opted to drive the Bombardier on the road so we could park the trailer at Tangles. Michael and I followed in Tinker's pickup while Tinker piloted the Bombardier, in fourth gear, down the shoulder of the road. The travois tree that had lasted for nearly two days cross-country peeled into blonde wood shavings as it dragged along the dark, wet pavement. I wondered if it would last until Tangles, or if we would be treated to a shower of sparks when the metal of the trailer scraped on the asphalt.

Just as we arrived at Tangles, Wayne pulled in from the opposite direction. A friend of his, Bill Scott, had driven him down the Parks Highway from Willow. They hadn't come yesterday because of the same snowstorm that had plagued us all day. It had blanketed the Parks Highway and had prompted travel advisories warning motorists to stay home unless they had an emergency. Wayne knew we could take care of ourselves, so he and Bill decided to wait out the storm.

"What happened to you guys?" he greeted us with a twinkly grin. "I thought you'd be out yesterday and today you'd be all clean and the cabin would be warm and you'd have a hot meal ready for me!" Then he looked at the trailer. "Holy Hell! Where's the wheel?" he exclaimed.

"It's in the trailer. We broke an axle early yesterday, and just got out today. I've gotta go back to get the rest of the gear and Zarnke's moose," Tinker replied, sounding weary at the prospect.

At the cabin, I cooked and made sandwiches and a thermos of hot coffee for Tinker. The men fueled the machine, loaded it on the truck, and by 4:00 p.m., Tinker was back on the trail heading for the gear and the moose stashed in the trailless snowy woods. It was a long hard run, not something a person looks forward to at the end of a season when what you really want is a nice hot bath.

Later, he told us he was about an hour away from the stashed gear by the time it had gotten too dark to drive. He pulled the machine next to a sheltering tree, put up a tarp and crawled into his sleeping bag for the night. The next day, the moose and gear took all the space in the back and the front of the machine. Tinker said he barely had room for himself in the middle driver's seat. One passenger's seat was stuffed to the ceiling, and the other side had only enough room for him to crawl over stuff in order to get in and out of the Bombardier.

A macho Alaska wilderness experience indeed! Although it was a trip filled with tension and cold and aching bone-deep from being wedged in the Bombardier so tightly, it is one of my best memories. It is a memory seared in the cold steel-blue colors of snowy hills backed by darker gray skies, burned deeply by the glow of the warming campfire outside the safe, dry green tent filled with cushiony boughs and drowsy hunters.

J. D.'s Swan Song

WITH THE HOT SIX-QUART pressure cooker (the Penny Pennington cooker) full of tomorrow's half-cooked dinner in hand, I bent slightly and pushed my way out through the white canvas tent door. I concentrated on not burning myself while I headed for the huge spruce tree about twenty feet away. The next day's evening meal was going to spend the night away from the tent. The evening air was cool, assuring that the food wouldn't spoil.

Motion must have caught my eye, because as I set the cooker at the base of the tree, I glanced first at the murky pond beyond the tree, then toward the trail that lead to camp.

"Eric!" I called to the other assistant guide. "That stupid black bear is back again! He's coming down the trail from the creek."

I'd left Eric Decker in the tent, fiddling with his video camera. His feet thumped across the old, gray plywood flooring as he headed for the door.

"Where?" Eric poked his tousled brown-haired head out the tent door and peered toward the trail, but the bear had moved close enough that the Bombardier temporarily blocked it from view.

"He's right there. You'll be able to see 'im in a couple seconds." I pointed, then abruptly realized that I was away from the tent and, more importantly, away from my rifle. A few quick steps found me standing next to Eric at the tent's door. The canvas walls suddenly looked mighty skimpy.

The bear didn't break stride or even turn his head when I yelled to Eric. Neither of us kept our voices low as the bear followed the trail's turn-around circle toward the tent. He casually swung his head to look at us as he shambled along the far side of the loop. This one was bold. A twinge of alarm made me shiver.

Most bears, black or grizzly, disappear at the sound of a loud voice, sometimes so quickly that you think you only imagined seeing them. Usually, the only way you know a bear is around is by seeing its tracks, quite often in the path you took a few hours earlier. Not so with this one. It showed disconcertingly distinct signs of being what's commonly called a nuisance, or "J. D." (short for juvenile delinquent) bear.

71

Eric dived into the tent for his iron-sighted .375—a good bear gun. I was hot on his heels, grabbing my 30.06 with the scope. My theory was two rifles are better than one. Back outside in seconds, we were in time to watch the fat black bear stride alongside the tent only eight feet away from us. He swung his head toward us for a slow glance, but wasn't interested. He wanted the Bombardier.

"I bet I know why he's after the Bomber," I muttered. "Remember last night? He thinks there's more meat."

Late yesterday, Eric and I had delivered hunters and their moose to the lake. After Wayne flew everyone and their meat out, we quickly rustled up dinner from a small chunk of moose we'd brought down from Point Camp. The night had been cool, so we put the remaining raw meat away from the tent, in the trailer attached to the Bombardier.

We set the meat outside for a reason. It's a good idea to store any kind of food away from your sleeping quarters to keep uninvited animal visitors away. In all the years I've hunted, bears have come in at night for hanging meat (some seasons more regularly than others), or during the day when no one was around. They have always left our food boxes alone. In fact, most bears leave humans alone. Those that aren't afraid of people generally mean trouble and are dangerous to the unwary. Those are the ones that must be killed for the safety of all involved. When that happens, you have to take the skull and hide to the local Alaska Department of Fish and Game office to be sealed and report what happened. They attach separate metal tags to the hide and skull, pull a tooth for aging, and fill out paperwork. I keep the skulls, cutting off as much meat as I can and then boiling them, first in plain water and then in Biz or Spic and Span to help finish getting the brains out and the cartilage off. My husband says I'm icky. But he cheerfully puts up with my house-decorating idiosyncracies, like lynx and bear skulls set among antiques, ivory, and crystal.

That evening Eric and I sat at the edge of the lake, scanning the hillsides with our binoculars and spotting scopes until dusk's velvety gray made it too dark to see. Lounging against a couple of tree trunks, we listened to the water lap against the lakeshore and admired the azure and rose sunset, watching the sky reflect in the ripply lake.

Island Lake, a favorite place of mine, has a white canvas wall tent pitched on a permanent plywood floor. Once in a while I get to spend a night alone with the water gently lapping at the lakeshore and a creek burbling not far away, which makes for a peaceful evening. These are good bath nights. I have the tent all to myself, I get to heat all the water I want on the Coleman stove, and I don't have to hurry. One small dishpan is good for a sponge-bath, and the small dishpan followed by another bucket of water lets me wash my hair too. Twenty days in the bush without a bath and shampoo gets to be too much.

Sunsets spread their alpenglow, or sometimes pale orchid and tangerine glory over the surface of the lake, helping me speed through rolls and rolls of film. One of my "sanity pictures" is of an Island Lake sunset. It's propped right next to my computer at work so I can lose myself on the lakeshore for a minute or two, where haunting cries of loons send me off to sleep and swans honking wake me up just after sunrise. Blueberries at the back of the tent give themselves up for delectable pancakes.

About 9:00 p.m. we lit the Coleman lantern in the tent to ready our gear for the night. Sleeping bags unrolled, we both checked our flashlights and rifles. Not only did we have the little bit of meat (enough for one decent roast) in the trailer, we also had a moose hide about twenty-five feet outside the tent door, between the big spruce and a small pond next to the lake.

Ordinarily, a moose hide wouldn't have been at this particular camp, since it's mainly a pick-up and drop-off camp. But this time a moose killed far afield had been gutted and brought back whole in the Bombardier trailer, to be skinned and quartered here. White sox, those pesky, squirmy, vicious little gnats that make you bleed and leave huge welts when they bite, were terrible the day we got that moose. Their fierce biting convinced us to load up the whole moose and head for the breeze at the lake.

Because one of the next group of hunters was after a grizzly bear, Wayne wanted the hide left there. His pre-season flying had shown grizzly bears to be scarce, so if one happened to come in for the hide, it would make for much easier hunting. I wasn't too concerned because in years past I'd spent many nights at this tent in peace and quiet, even with moose pieces hanging nearby. The only disturbances then had been caused by a resident ermine, and by an owl that once tried to land on the smoking stovepipe. With the rifles on the floor next to our cots, shells in the chambers and safeties on, we put out the light, snuggled in our bags, and drifted quickly off to sleep.

About midnight, our slumber was broken, and we were both suddenly wide awake. But neither of us knew why.

"Sharon." Eric's hushed voice came from the end of the tent. "Are you awake?"

"Yes. Did you hear something?"

"I don't know. Let's listen."

A few moments went by, with both of us trying to breathe as shallowly as possible so no slippery sleeping bag noise would keep us from hearing the night noises outside the tent. I tried to separate the breeze-on-the-brush noise from what might be heavy animal footfalls.

"Did you make a noise?" Eric sounded startled.

"Yeah. My stomach grumbled," I said quietly. No sooner had I finished the sentence, though, than we both heard the metallic clank of the trailer's tailgate. An animal was after that little bit of meat in the trailer!

"Hey! Get outta there, you asshole! Go away! Scram!" Gut reaction made us both yell. For some reason, calling a bear or other night marauding creature an asshole or a son-of-a-bitch makes you feel tougher. Sometimes you need that feeling.

We scrambled out of our sleeping bags and grabbed our rifles. I held the big flashlight, first shining it toward the end of the trailer, then swinging the beam in wide, slow arcs to see if any gleaming green eyeballs would appear. Nothing. We checked the trailer. The heavy cardboard box the meat was in hadn't been disturbed, and the ground was covered with blueberry bushes that hid any tracks.

"Huh. Whatever it was, it left the meat alone. S'pose it was a bear?" I asked. I was sure it was a bear, but wanted to believe that it wasn't.

"Maybe. It could be something smaller, though. Couldn't be the ermine from under the tent. He's too small to make that noise. Maybe a fox jumped in the trailer, and then left when we yelled." Eric didn't sound positive about his theory.

As always happens in this kind of situation, nerves dictated that we both attend to nature's call before we went back to sleep. The trail to the outhouse went around behind the tent, about thirty feet down the lake's shoreline. I did my best to walk slowly and calmly, but cold prickles down my back made my skin jump. I just knew the bear was waiting for me on the other side of the outhouse, which is only two small spruce trees resting on a dirt bank with a toilet seat nailed across them—no roof or walls. The only shelter is from the boughs of the large spruce that the outhouse is backed up against.

With my rifle propped against my leg, I shined the flashlight in erratic semi-circles as I sat on the cold seat. Then, in "what's-behind-me" haste, I scampered back to the tent where Eric stood guard with his rifle. It was his turn to visit the outhouse, and it made me feel better seeing his flashlight-waving pattern copying mine. I always feel better when I know I'm not the only one who's nervous.

Again in the tent, our keen senses of hearing sharpened by that clank, we stayed awake for a little while. We finally slipped into slumber, only to be startled awake at 2:30 in the morning, and then again at 5:00. Each time we yelled, including obscenities in our barrage of noise. Each time, the animal left, but the 5:00 departure was prolonged. The grunting and rustling that accompanied the last visit left us both positive that our visitor was a bear. A persistent one, at that.

Up at 7:00 because our edgy nerves wouldn't let us sleep, we investigated before eating breakfast, while the freshly stoked wood stove took the night's chill off the tent. The meat was gone. The box was on the ground, but the Safeway plastic bags and the two-gallon Ziploc bag the meat had been in were nowhere to be found. We looked briefly for tracks and found some fairly large black bear prints. The claws, which showed sharply in the dirt, were close to the toe-pads, so we knew our visitor wasn't a grizzly. It also helped to explain the quiet; grizzlies usually snort and mutter when they come in.

After French toast with maple syrup and some stout coffee, Eric took his rifle and scrounged around the bushes beyond the trail, hoping to find plastic bag remnants. He did. They were tattered, and not a bite of moose meat was left.

Because the new hunters weren't due in until the next day, we had an entire day to spruce up camp, grease the Bombardier, and make ourselves a little more presentable. A week's worth of bush living adds some unusual aromas to your persona.

During the day we talked about our intrepid bear. He acted almost as though he was accustomed to handouts and to humans. But that didn't make sense, because we were hunting in an extremely unpopulated area. The only way to get there year-round was by bush plane, all-terrain vehicle in the summer, or snow machine or dog team in the winter. I'd never seen anyone who walked in. Sometimes there are nuisance or rogue bears that are purely dangerous, and that must be shot to avoid harm to people. We thought this one could be a nuisance bear and that we might end up having to shoot it. The idea was sobering. It's one thing to hunt, but entirely another to have to kill something you don't want to just so you can assure safety. The outcome would depend on how the bear acted if it came in camp again. We hoped J. D., as we had taken to calling him, wouldn't come back. The meat was all gone, so if J. D. was typical, his nose would tell him there was no need to visit again, and he would do one of the things bears do best: avoid humans.

Eric was nervous about the moose hide being so close to the tent after the previous night's escapades, so I towed it away with the Bombardier. We figured any animal interested in it would follow the scent and would stay away from the tent, especially since the fresh meat was gone.

When we returned, I parked the Bombardier with the nose of the machine on slightly higher ground and the tracks straddling a dip, which would make my job of scooting on my back underneath to grease all the fittings much easier. Ordinarily, it had only about eighteen inches of clearance, but this gave me two feet, meaning my shoulders wouldn't be so scrunched up.

As we puttered around camp, we half-expected to hear the airplane, because hunters often arrive at the Tangle Lakes base camp a day early in their eagerness, and Wayne flies them in so they can get a jump on their ten-day hunts. Since it's illegal for anyone to hunt the same day they're airborne, an extra day can mean a lot.

No one appeared, though, so we luxuriated in our day off from dawn-to-dusk hosting, guiding, and cooking pressures. We even got in a small bath after all the chores were done. The sponge bath felt wonderful, and so did clean hair, even though the cool breeze was able to waft through it after all the grime was gone.

In the tent later that evening, we played with the video camera. Eric wanted to have it ready to film the arrival of the hunters. Also, since the next day was

Eric's anniversary, he planned to surprise his wife Shelley with an anniversary segment of tape. I began dinner for the next day's onslaught of people while Eric checked the camera batteries and found the end of his latest taping segment.

"Sharon," he said, "say something. You're on camera, live at hunting camp!"

I got a little silly and did a French chef version of "Julia Child of Island Lake." I sat on the cot with the pressure cooker lid in my lap and the pot on the floor in front of me, slicing up garden-fresh carrots, cabbage, and onions for a thick soup that would be tomorrow night's dinner. Waving my knife for emphasis, I chopped food, opened cans, gabbled in a bad imitation French accent about how a camp chef prepares food, and prattled about my fine cooking.

"Watch very closely ze technique with ze knife! You must always use ze same knife for onions as for meat. Ze flavor holds better."

In went a few cans of peas, corn, stewed tomatoes, and green beans, along with the chopped-up remainder of the roast that had been last night's dinner.

"Ze cook always strives for excellent flavor," I proclaimed, tossing in minced garlic, a few chopped-up slices of canned bacon and dousing everything with Worcestershire sauce before adding water.

"Notice ze twist of ze wrist when I pour ze sauce. Zees is very critical to ze culinary result," I said, demonstrating as I spoke.

A few minutes on the Coleman stove brought the concoction to a rolling boil. Then I snugged down the lid and headed out the door for the big tree. That's when I saw the roly-poly black bear, on its way back to pay us another visit, and yelled for Eric.

"Well, now what?" I asked, as Eric and I stood side by side in front of the tent.

"Let's see how close he gets to us," replied Eric.

The fat blackie strolled unconcernedly past.

"If he doesn't leave when we yell, we better shoot 'im," said Eric, just as I was saying, "We gotta get rid of this one."

We yelled and roared. I got two metal pots and clanged them together. The bear didn't go away. Instead, he reared up and snuffled in the back of the Bombardier.

"Hey, get outta there! Git, you!" I howled.

"Scram. Go away! Yaaaah!" yelled Eric.

All our efforts were to no avail. The bear ignored us, not even deigning to glance our direction. Finding nothing interesting, he dropped to all fours, went to the front of the machine, and almost crawled into the cab. That made me angry, so I yelled again.

"Don't you dare, you asshole! Hiyaa! Git!"

He slowly sank to the ground and made his way around the front of the machine and tried to crawl in the opposite side of the cab. All our discussions had been much louder than conversational voices; we'd yelled at the bear and he hadn't been at all fazed. And he'd walked within ten feet of us, showing no fear.

"As soon as he's back in sight I think we oughta shoot. This isn't safe," said Eric.

"Yeah, we got hunters coming in, plus it wouldn't be too smart to spend all night with that thing around," I replied.

Turning to face the Bombardier and trailer, Eric began to lift his rifle to his shoulder.

"Eric, if you shoot that machine, Wayne'll kill you," I cautioned him. "He'll probably kill me, too." He nodded his head.

The bear investigated the trailer. Finally, he dropped to all fours and walked out from behind the shelter of the metal trailer toward the tree and the pond. Rifles blazed, the flash of fire from each barrel temporarily blinding us. The bear sprang forward toward the tree, and we both shot again. Even though it was almost dark, we were sure the bear was hit because of the "whump" sound the bullets made. In a twinkling, the bear did a button-hook turn, took a flying leap, and soared with a spread-eagled bellyflop straight into the shallow, soft-bottomed pond.

After the big splash, all was quiet. Eric and I hurried nervously to the edge of the pond and peered through the rapidly gathering night blackness at the inky water. Everything appeared completely still. Then the bear gasped his last and several air bubbles burbled up. Neither Eric nor I had seen a bear die in a pond before.

After recovering from the quivers caused by shooting the unpredictable critter, we grumped about what a nuisance the bear had been.

"Y'know, Eric," I said, "it figures this fool thing would die in a puddle. He started out as trouble, and he finished off as trouble."

"Yeah. I wonder why he behaved so strangely," said Eric. "Most bears wouldn't have gotten so close to us. He showed absolutely no fear, coming in when it's still light. And he should have skedaddled when we yelled. I've been around a lotta bears and this one was the weirdest."

I agreed, then paused, realizing we had a good bit of work ahead of us. "Now we've gotta skin him in the dark. We can't let the meat spoil. How are we gonna get him out of the water?"

"I guess I'll see how deep the pond is." Eric took a stick, and found out the water was only about three feet deep. He waded in and felt around until he grasped a paw. He pulled, and the bear floated right up. We tugged him onto dry land, and I went to fill the Coleman lantern and gather our skinning gear.

The five and one-half foot bear had a thick, glossy coat, so we took special care to get all the fat off the inner side of the hide, and worked slowly and diligently to keep from accidentally poking a hole in the hide. We took turns holding the lantern and skinning. Around midnight the job was done and our backs ached. Quickly hanging the whole bear on the meat pole, we draped the hide, fur side down, over a make-shift table. We left skinning the feet and head until daylight. Pitch-black night was no time for that kind of tedious work.

I thought about the tender roasts this fat bear would make, then giggled.

"What's so funny?" asked Eric.

"What goes around comes around! This guy ate our meat, now we get to eat him."

Pressure-Cooked Barbecue Bear

5 lb. bear roast
6–8 cloves garlic, chopped
3 celery ribs, chopped
2 large onions, chopped
1 Tbsp. olive oil
½ tsp. each oregano & basil
¼ cup parsley flakes
your favorite BBQ sauce, or: 1 cup catsup, ¼ cup vinegar, ¼ cup Worcestershire sauce, and ½ cup brown sugar

Saute onions, garlic, and celery in olive oil until onions are translucent. Add the bear roast, spices and BBQ sauce. Carrots are also an excellent addition to this concoction. Pressure cook according to your cooker's directions, usually around 15–20 minutes. Pour cold water over the cooker to cool immediately. If you're in camp and don't have cold water, reduce cooking time to 10 minutes and allow the cooker to cool until the pressure plug wiggles freely. Serve with rice, potatoes, or macaroni.

Bear Tracks, Full and Empty

I N HIS BOOK *Longbows in the North,* E. Donnall Thomas, Jr. describes his hunts with a bow in Alaska and Siberia. He says, "Those venturing into the American wilderness have always had an uneasy relationship with bears, especially in Alaska where bear stories are always near the epicenter of regional myth" (p. 96).

Thomas' narratives on grizzly and black bear behavior around humans put me in mind of my own experiences. Since I've shared some of those episodes in this book, I should perhaps add a little perspective. Until I totted up a list of bear encounters, I hadn't realized that every year, save a few in my late teens, has been defined by some bear activity. I should also add that I'm in my late forties now and have never been bitten, swatted, or even seriously charged by a bear, grizzly or black. That's during a childhood spent mostly outdoors on our Alaskan homestead, in an area that is a known bear migration corridor; a lifetime of hunting; and several years of guiding. Encounters, yes. Inquisitive inspections, yes. Life-threatening, maybe. Attacks, no. I am wary of bears—but not paralyzed with fright or irrationally scared. I do give them serious respect.

How to avoid nasty encounters? Being observant and aware of your surroundings helps. So does using your senses—sight, sound, and smell. Watch for fluid, rolling movement; listen for the tiniest crunch of a twig breaking; and your nose will tell you all about the rank smell of a grizzly. The odor is both distinct and hair-raising. It means that you are close (very close, since human noses aren't as sensitive as animal noses and thus don't warn us any too quickly) and that you had best—quickly—retrace your steps, and find some avenue that affords better visibility than thick brush.

There are a few wise "you-shoulds" to adhere to for personal safety: keep meat-hanging poles away from where you sleep and keep food away from your sleeping quarters. A couple of happenstances one season will illustrate why.

During the September 1994 moose season, many bears were around—lots more than normal. When we arrived on the first spotting hill with the Bombardier—where we always stop for a look before heading the last mile to the Point Camp cabin—the first thing I saw on the Red Knobs across the valley was a big blonde sow grizzly with two roly-poly cubs bouncing along behind her. Everywhere we went throughout the season, we saw different bear tracks, often just hours old, since their tracks usually covered ours.

A large grizzly stole the head of a moose, antlers still attached, from the site where a moose had been shot. Mike Tinker and Dan Cox, the hunter's father, found the head about a hundred yards away. The bear was obviously large—both of Tinkers' size 10 ½ feet fit in a single bear track, with length to spare. It had tugged the head and antlers through alders so thick the men had to crawl and wiggle to find the head, much less retrieve it. But retrieve it they did, and they brought it back to Point Camp with the rest of the meat, a little of which had been munched and slobbered on. (Quick knife work took care of that.)

Two days later at Point Camp, a grizzly pulled the entire camp meatpole down on top of itself—loaded with about seven hundred pounds of moose. The pole, about seventy-five yards from the cabin, was twelve feet off the ground, which meant that the moose pieces were about seven feet off the ground. The pole and the meat lying in the dirt said very clearly: this Interior grizzly was not little. We also had a pretty good idea what time the bear had come in: several of us woke up about a quarter after four that morning, a little surprised that others were awake too. At the time, we joked about all the coffee everybody drank before going to bed. Later, we agreed that the thump of the meat pole landing on the ground was the wake-up catalyst.

We surmised that the bear, determined to get the meat, had tracked it to the meat pole. Since none of the meat had been touched, we gathered that the pole and all its weight must have landed on the grizzly with a stunning thud, startling it. Since the hunters were flying out that day, we simply loaded the moose into the Bombardier and headed for Island Lake. After the hunters left, Don Cameron and I hung up the remaining meat to be flown out the next day. We wondered briefly if the bear would track the meat to the lake, shrugged, and headed for Point Camp. We planned to give the camp a good cleaning before going in the Bombardier the next day to retrieve other hunters and deliver them to a prearranged float plane pick-up at a different lake. Harley McMahan, a high-school friend and owner of a local air taxi service, was doing the flying. Despite a tight schedule, he always managed to be pretty much on time, even early, spurred by a seemingly endless supply of Mountain Dew. We wanted to have the hunters there and ready for him.

We did as much as we could that evening, had dinner and a cup of Crown Royal, and turned in. At precisely 4:18 (I checked my Timex Ironman Indiglo watch) the next morning I awoke in the velvety black of the dark cabin. The sixth sense that I trust very much told me that something was different, and probably wrong. I lay in my sleeping bag, barely breathing, listening very hard. I thought I heard something brush against the back wall of the log cabin, which my bunk was attached to. Raising up on one elbow, I held my breath. Yes, something was indeed brushing against the exterior of the cabin, and it was large.

"Don," I said tightly, "we've got company." I shoved my glasses on, after fumblingly retrieving them from their hard-sided case nested in the neck-collar tubing of my sleeping bag. I wriggled out of my bag, grabbing the .416 from the floor where I'd placed it the night before, shell in the chamber and safety on, then my flashlight. Although the meat was at Island Lake, I had figured the bear might be back to the cabin for a nocturnal visit, since that was the last place it knew the meat was. Why did I have to be right?

I could hear Don getting out of his bunk, and soon he was beside me, rifle in hand. I flicked my flashlight on and set it on the small table, facing it toward the door. It's not a good idea to blind yourself by looking into the beam of a flashlight when you really need to see your adversary.

"Is it still out there?" he whispered. In response, a jerry can and a 30-gallon metal storage barrel clanked and banged at the side of the cabin.

"Get outta here!" I yelled.

Harley McMahan picking up hunters at Caribou Lake, September 1996.

We stood, feet wide apart, in what Pete Buist calls "a high state of alert," waiting for the next development. For a while, it was still beside the cabin. We heard tree branches scrape the cabin's log wall, then more metal cans banging about. We yelled.

Then the bear was on the porch, thumping and banging. I imagined the grizzly with my frame backpack in its arms. Don and I yelled again. It didn't leave.

I grabbed a saucepan and clanged it on the wood stove. Big deal, according to the bear: it responded by clanging something on the porch. The door to the cabin swings in, so all the bear had to do was lean on it. I was fervently wishing for a back door, or even an exit through the roof. Later, Don said he was wishing for a generator with lots of floodlights outside, so we could flip a breaker to light the area. (Until a visiting bear gets used to it, hanging a lit Coleman lantern outside is a good deterrent. Bears will circle, but will typically stay away until they figure out that the light is harmless.)

I flicked the .416's safety off, telling Don that I had done so. We agreed that if the door so much as moved, we would both shoot. The cabin shook a little as the bear continued its inventory of our belongings on the porch. So I rained saucepan blows on the metal stove again, screaming and yelling the whole time. Finally, the porch area was quiet.

"Well, are you ready for this?" I asked Don as I reached for the door to pull it open. "How 'bout if you shine the flashlight so I can shoot if that thing is still there?"

Don agreed. Once the door was open, Don quickly swept the "front yard" with the flashlight beam. I took the light and went out on the porch, beaming the light slowly around the yard again, as well as the trail past the wall tent just below the cabin. The bear was still there: it whoofed a couple times. The brush rustled; then all was still. It was after 5:00 a.m.—the bear had entertained us for over half an hour.

We decided that sleep was out of the question. Since I had the .416 with open sights, I manned the flashlight and stood guard while Don tossed stove wood inside and grabbed the lantern fuel. We had decided that if we had to be awake, we might as well be comfortable. Besides, smoke from the chimney would be a deterrent, as would Coleman light shining through the window.

As soon as it was light outdoors, we looked for tracks and surveyed the damage. There were no tracks around the cabin—too many fallen leaves—and tracks by the meat pole weren't discernable from those that had been there before. The grizzly hadn't done any real damage. Cans were knocked over, and bloodied boards stashed at the back of the cabin had been gnawed on.

We discovered that two of the coolers had a couple packages of rotten meat in them. Frozen burger had been brought from town; it had thawed and had not been eaten. Once the bear discovered the meat at the pole was gone, its nose probably said: "go down hill, something smells pretty good;" and sent it directly to us. We took the rotten meat to dispose of along the way, then thoroughly washed the coolers with soap and hot water. After the clean-up, we agreed that next fall's shopping list would include Clorox, Pine-Sol, and vinegar.

Later, Don allowed as how, when he heard me say we had "company," he had taken his baseball cap from the nail on the wall above his bunk, and put it on. It seemed, after all, the polite thing to do. Then, during a potty stop on our way to pick up the other hunters, I discovered that I, too, had done something nearly as silly. I had to tell Don why I was laughing: "Guess what! I still have my jammies on!" In the excitement, I had pulled my jeans on over the long johns which, to that point, had been my pajama bottoms.

I've learned that after a serious bear encounter my butt and thigh muscles quiver in a few minutes of a palsy-like fit. It seems to go like this: tense up—adrenalin rush—fight or flight kicks in—threat resolves itself—adrenalin drains—palsy sets in. And it's pretty easy to get giddy giggles as another tension relief mechanism. Remember the chapter on J. D.? Well, that's what happened just after he dove in the pond. And, to a lesser degree, that's what happened when the bear made its 4:18 a.m. visit to the cabin.

Bears are intelligent creatures—case in point is: in 1996, we used the Bombardier, which had been parked for several days, to go get water at a nearby spring. It was about a three-mile round trip. An hour and sixty-five gallons of water later, we were back at camp. The next morning, we discovered large grizzly tracks going straight to the meat pole, then turning around and leaving. We used the machine again several days later to get to a different hunting area; once more, the grizzly checked the meat pole, except this time it happened in the early evening during the hour-long visit Tinker and I made to the Point for some last-minute glassing. That bear had learned from the previous season (or seasons?) that the Bombardier sound was supposed to mean meat on that meatpole. The realization certainly gave us pause.

So much for current bear stories. Except for the years I didn't hunt because college conflicted with moose season, bears have dogged my footsteps all my life.

My very first memory of a bear is not really mine. I was an active participant, but too young to recall any of the circumstances except the beginning and getting in trouble at the end. It's my parents' story and they repeated it enough that I know it too.

It seems that Marian, the woman across the road—part of the three-family group who migrated from Michigan to homestead near each other—had gone berry picking. Her son Raymond wanted to find her, and I assured him that I knew where she had gone.

I recall it being a sunny afternoon, and I can see in my mind's eye the log house with the bark still on the logs and tow-headed Raymond in the yard, between the house and the outhouse covered with green asphalt roofing paper.

Raymond and I set out on the logging trail that I, in my three-year-old mind, was certain Marian had followed. We didn't find her and somehow got off the trail. We emerged some time later a half-mile up the road. We brightly told the anxious parents (Marian had come home, with berries and no kids) who had been yelling and yelling, that we saw a nice black doggie by a big stump. They blanched. No one had a black doggie, and no one else lived near, so no stray could have wandered in. We had obviously been quite near a black bear. I got a lecture, and so ended my first guiding experience.

The next vivid memory also involves berries, a black bear, a dog, and a mom—my mother, this time. My little sister, Roberta, then about one, was asleep across the road at Queenie and Bill's house. Mother snatched the opportunity to go pick berries, and took me with her. Given where we were along one of the logging trails my father had created while collecting house logs for the three families, we must have been picking cranberries.

The author's foot next to a grizzly track, early 1990s. That track wasn't there last night! Most likely it's a sow with a cub; note the smaller track at the lower left.

Our dog Buzzy, a female boxer and malamute mix, was with us. She had some malamute traits—white hair, long nose, and a strong, medium sized, graceful body—and other boxer parts—short hair, brown eyes, and a very tenacious, protective personality. Her ears, twisting, turning, expressive barometers, were a decided mix: shaped like boxer ears and thin, but pointed and upright like a malemute's. Buzzy was intelligent and sensitive—except when it came to porcupines. She always came home with a snoot-full of quills.

Mother and I had picked a while, then worked our way out of the brush back onto the logging trail. We heard Buzzy raising quite a ruckus some distance below the trail. Mother decided Buzzy must have encountered a bear—she was using the bark reserved for bears or buffalo. The dog had a communication repertoire to convey the seriousness or urgency of a situation, and a series of sighs that registered pleasure, aggravation, or sheer disgust. Her language this time was serious and urgent.

We set out at a fast pace for home, staying on the Cletrac-built trail, which was cleared and easy walking. Suddenly, a black bear materialized in front of us. Buzzy burst out of the brush between us and the bear, at full bark, lunging and nipping at it. She was herding it away from us. As dog and bear dashed back into the brush below the trail, Mother and I turned and headed back in the direction we'd come from. Again, the bear popped out in the trail, blocking our path, again with Buzzy running interference. Mother and I turned once more in the direction of home. Once more, the bear intervened, and once again Buzzy was between us, going crazy. Dog and bear dove into the brush a third time. The fourth time we saw the bear, we were nearly nose-to-nose. I recall a long brown snout, and a bare ring around its neck, as though a collar had worn away the fur. Mother decided that was enough. She flung the berry bucket, grabbed my left hand and headed straight north toward the highway. I flapped in the breeze beside her—I don't think my feet touched the ground until we hit pavement. Although we'd gone about three-quarters of a mile from the house, we were only about a quarter of a mile from the paved road, since the logging trail generally paralleled the road.

Mother lost her hair-combs in the trees, but she didn't care. She wanted distance between us and that persistent, troublesome bear. Today's common wisdom of not running when confronted by a bear must not have been so common forty years ago—Mother certainly ran.

We hurried straight to Queenie's house, who fixed us a cup of tea and listened wide-eyed to our story. Mother didn't seem concerned about our ordeal, once she regained her breath from our dash through the brush and down the road. We laughed about the bear wearing Mother's hair-combs, and about how my left arm would always be longer than my right. Even today, it's a family joke.

We were proud of Buzzy's protective behavior. When she soon appeared, panting and pink tongue lolling out, we praised her and petted her. She seemed pleased with her afternoon's efforts.

Then Queenie's black cat jumped on Mother's lap, startling her so badly that her composure abruptly dissolved—she shrieked and burst into tears. The bear encounter had unnerved her. That was my first indication that bears were scary.

Several years later on a sunny summer afternoon, Buzzy treed a rotund black bear in Queenie's front yard while Mother, Roberta, and I visited, having cookies and tea. We got to Queenie's kitchen window next to her wood cookstove just in time to see the bear scrambling up the large spruce tree next to the squat log garage, about fifty feet away.

Buzzy's frenzied barking and jumping sent the bear scrabbling higher in the tree. As it went higher, the limbs it used for leverage to haul itself up got skinnier. One limb, about twenty feet up, was too thin and brittle. It broke, tumbling the bear to the ground. It landed with a thump we could hear inside the kitchen. For a moment, we wondered if the bear was dead. It lay motionless, shiny black hair glistening in the sun, as Buzzy darted in and out, a creamy, nipping blur. When the blackie made a horrible wheezing sound, we realized it had the wind knocked out of it. The bear stayed put for a few more minutes, then got up and staggered off, ignoring Buzzy.

In the late summer of 1956, Roberta and I were visiting Paul and Clare at Atlasta House for the day. As was our wont, we were climbing the steep hill immediately behind their combined lodge and home, playing in the heavy forest and running pell-mell down the hill, stopping ourselves by running into the back of the house. Suddenly, the four of us realized we weren't alone! A sow black bear and twin cubs were right behind us. We roared into the house through the back door, yelling in fright. John—or Marcy, I can't remember which—grabbed a rifle. When the bears didn't leave, they were dispatched. Just to be on the safe side, we played in the open front yard for quite a while.

Later, after Sue was born, we three girls decided to walk up the road about a quarter of a mile to visit Gert Lamier, another of the original group who had migrated from Michigan. Since it had rained most of the day, we were antsy, ready to do anything to get out of the house. Outdoors smelled fresh and green and clean. The pavement on the road even smelled good. Roberta and I walked along, Sue in the middle, toddling along as we each held a hand. About a third of the way to Gert's, we saw a black dog ambling from the ditch up the bank to the road. Suddenly we realized we were walking toward a black bear! Roberta and I spun and ran for home, Sue's hands still gripped in ours. Only when we got inside our house did we realize she no longer had her diapers. We had taken off so fast that her heavy cloth diapers and plastic overpants were left in a pile on the road. Mother didn't believe we had seen a bear—she thought we were pulling her leg. She changed her tune, though, when she got part way down the driveway and saw the bear across the road on the opposite bank. Those diapers stayed put for a while longer.

Our family used to buy cases of eggs to last us over the winter; come spring, a case or two would be so thoroughly rotten that the eggs were green or black inside when you cracked them open. The horribly putrid smell could make you take a couple steps backward. Those cases would be buried at the end of the sawmill so we could watch the grizzlies dig them up and roll in them. Some of the salmon carcasses also got buried there, for the same reason. We used to plaster

Roberta McLeod (left) and the author with the bears killed at Atlasta House, 1956.

our faces to the south living room window, watching the bears reveling in their stinky find.

Salmon drying on the clothesline (this was a multi-purpose clothes line—it doubled as a fish drying rack) was too much of a temptation for one bear. It cruised right between us—we were working on the outside of the greenhouse and Daddy was next to the powerhouse, about ten feet from the drying fish—to snag fish off the line. In one fluid move, it reared up, swept left to right, then right to left, dropped down to all fours and disappeared into the brush, not dropping a single fish. We weren't quick enough to see whether the bear stuffed the fish into its mouth or somehow had them corralled by one front leg. Needless to say, we were one dumbfounded family.

Queenie and Bill used to put dinner leftovers on the ground in front of their house so they could watch birds and four-legged critters, like foxes, that came in to sample the food. One day, though, they got a grizzly. Again, we were over for tea and cookies—it was our "job" to get their mail from the mailbox at the road and deliver it to them—a daily event (except for weekends) when school was out. By the time we realized it was there, the grizzly was sitting on its hind end, legs stretched out in front, looking for all the world like a furry brown Buddha. He wiped the peas, mashed potatoes, and gravy off the ground, first with one front paw, then the other, and alternately licked them clean with a very wide, light pink tongue. Finally, Bill decided it would be best to scare it off, so he went out and shot into the ground next to the bear, spraying it with gravel. Quicker than we could blink, that bear dove into the brush. It must have decided the yard-lunch was risky business, because it never reappeared.

One evening, Daddy looked out our north living room window at Bill and Queenie's house across the road, and was astonished to see a black bear on their kitchen porch. He opened our living room door and yelled; the bear ignored him. He got his rifle and marched across the road, yelling and gesticulating as he went. The bear, which looked like a blackie, ran off, but only a little way. Then it started to amble toward him. Enough of this, he thought, and shot it. It turned out to be a very old glacier bear, a blue variety that normally occurs in the Southeast Alaska, around Juneau. Since Alaska wasn't a state yet, he called the Fish and Wildlife Service. They took the bear, and it ended up in the Smithsonian for a while.

Another summer, Daddy shot a black bear off our tin can pile about seventy-five yards below the house. Paul and Clare, our friends from Atlasta House, were visiting for the day, so we all piled onto the sled when Daddy fired up the Cletrac to go get the bear. The plan was to bring it up to the house to skin it, so it would be closer to the meathouse. The guts that remained would get buried at the end of the sawmill so we could do our evening grizzly-watching.

At the tin can pile, Daddy parked the Cletrac and sled beside the bear. We pulled the side boards off the sled, rolled the bear on, and re-did the side boards. Daddy, rifle lying beside him on the running board of the Cletrac, took off. Paul, Clare, Roberta, and I had piled on top of the bear for the ride back to the house. Although the Cletrac was so loud Daddy couldn't hear us when we yelled, he knew something was up when all four of us streaked past him, wild-eyed. He stopped in time to see the bear getting to its feet on the sled. Quickly grabbing the rifle, he dispatched it with a close-range shot. Later, he said that was a good reminder to always give an "insurance" shot.

We learned a few years ago from a Fish and Game employee who bought our house and part of our homestead that our homestead was in a bear migratory area for both blacks and grizzlies, which finally explained why we saw so many more bears than other people when we were growing up. Back then, even Fish

Bruce McLeod, daughter Roberta, dog Buzzy, and the glacier bear that was shot just off Queenie Bourdeau's porch in 1958.

and Game didn't know why there were so many bears, just that we seemed to have the corner on the market.

One fall, a particularly persistent grizzly adopted our meathouse. The eight-foot-by-ten-foot meathouse was built out of eight-inch, three-sided logs, layered four feet high and spiked together with bridge spikes. The peaked roof was supported by four-inch-by-four-inch posts. Small-gauge screen kept the bugs out, and chain-link fence material surrounded the outside of the small-gauge screen. Those posts and chain-link fencing were a mere annoyance to the bear. We awoke one late, dark August night to the most god-awful snarling and coughing at the meathouse. We could hear the chain-link fence rattling, then more roaring and whoofing. Daddy shot once with the .45-70. The bear whoofed a couple more times, and silence descended. We decided to go look in the morning after it got light.

Even before the coffee perked, we all dashed to the meathouse, Daddy with the .45-70, just in case. The grizzly had decimated the south side of the meathouse. The logs were intact, but the four-by-four posts were out and the chain-link fencing was mashed flat. The bear had reached to the top of it, most likely hooked it with his claws, and pulled it down. After it got into the meathouse and pulled down a hind quarter, it must have had trouble trying to go back out the same way. The door, which opened out and had been latched, was flat on the ground. The grizzly had walked it off its hinges and ruined the latch.

We worked that morning making the meathouse functional again. Fortunately, we had enough chain-link fencing to go around twice; this time, we used bigger nails on the four-by-fours.

Several days later, Mother and us three girls went to the State Fair in Palmer. We stayed to watch Dr. Zhivago at the Palmer movie theater, then drove the 123 miles home. Fittingly, the first forty or so miles were in a mist so thick we were reduced to thirty-mile-an-hour driving. It was about 2:30 in the morning when we rounded the corner to the downhill straight stretch about a mile from home, where we could catch the first glimpse of the house. We could see the porch light was on, a cue that something was wrong. Daddy didn't burn electricity needlessly, and he wouldn't have left it on for us. Ordinary when arriving home in the dark, we would leave the car headlights on long enough for one of us to get in the house to turn the porch light on. Seeing it on made us nervous.

About a month earlier, a mile and a half from our house, a traveler stopped to help some men who had the hood of their car up and was beaten, robbed, and tied up for his kindness. We'd been gone fishing, and when we got home, we found blood on our doorstep. We thought the dog had cut his foot, and didn't think anything more about it until later in the evening when Marcy White called to tell us what had happened. The man had gotten loose and had crawled through the bushes, afraid that the men would come back and find him. They had told him they would shoot him if they found out he had moved from where they'd left him. It was his blood on our porch. When we weren't home, he had crawled the two miles to Marcy's. He did that rather than cross the road to Bill and Queenie's house, afraid that he might be seen in the open expanse of our two driveways.

Needless to say, Mother and us girls were on edge. Mother shut off the head-lights about a half-mile before the house, and turned off the car in the driveway so there would be no engine noise. Figuring the rain would mask any crunching the tires would make on the gravel, we rolled to a stop by the kitchen porch. I slunk out of the car and peeked in the kitchen window. There sat Daddy, smoking a cigarette and drinking a cup of coffee. He didn't look happy, but he was alone. We piled out of the car and dashed into the house.

"What's wrong? What are you doing up?" we asked.

"That God-damned bear was back," Daddy replied, glowering.

"Why are you mad?" we wanted to know.

"Come look," he said. He grabbed the flashlight and led us outside. We followed him off the porch to the sawmill. When he played the flashlight beam over the sawmill blade, we understood immediately why he was unhappy.

He told us the bear woke him up about 2:00 a.m., not too long before we arrived. He decided this was it for the bear. He jacked a shell into the .45-70 and snuck out the living room door. He stealthily moved along the back of the house, then around the corner. He saw a huge, hulking shape in the rain, in line with the meathouse. He took careful aim, fired, and was promptly deafened by an immense, resounding metallic "GOOONNNGGG." He had blasted a hole in the circular, four-foot high sawmill blade, ruining the blade. The bullet-hole was about three inches in diameter, and the backside peeled back jaggedly, looking much like a flower that had blossomed badly.

It would be very difficult to repair, but repair it Daddy did, with his acetylene and oxygen torches, heating the metal, pounding the jagged parts back in, heating it some more and pounding again, over and over. Finally, the blade spun true and went back on the mill. And strangely, the grizzly never came back. Daddy figured since bears hear so well, that the grizzly decided to stay away from that awful noise even though the treasure trove of meat was still there.

Sometimes, when you have a good, safe observation point, it's fun to watch bears. Other times, you feel like maybe, just maybe, you're the dinner entree of choice.

Anything can happen when bears enter the picture. A very common saying among those familiar with them is: "The only predictable thing about a bear is that they are very unpredictable." Remembering that and keeping your wits about you are about the best you can do.

The sawmill blade with the repaired hole from Bruce McLeod's .45-70.

Bowhunting With Muzzy

John Musacchia passed away on July 1, 1997.

JOHN MUSACCHIA IS A BOWHUNTER who hunted many years with Wayne and Tinker and who was a hunting partner of Fred Bear, founder of Bear Archery. John is what's known as a "traditionalist"—that is, he doesn't use a compound bow. Compounds have too many pulleys and too much string and need to be tuned too regularly for his taste. His first bow, the Kodiak by Fred Bear Archery, was given to him by his wife Barbara in the 1950s after rifle hunting lost its challenge. In recent times, he shoots a recurve. John aims instinctively and shoots quickly. He believes very strongly in the purity of the bow hunting sport and thus has no use for aiming or sighting contraptions or other mechanical devices as substitutes for practice and skill. His hunting skills are such that he easily gets within forty yards or less of the animal he's seeking. As a result, working with him is infinitely more pleasurable than dealing with the hurry-scurry of many rifle hunters. I like spending the time to get closer to the animals, waiting if the shot's not good, or backing off completely. I like that the shooting method is less startling to the animal, that it's quiet.

Skilled, ethical bow and rifle hunters respect their quarry and do their utmost to assure a clear, true shot. They aim for the lung and heart area to achieve their most effective shot. The difference is, arrows don't make an animal panic and run the way bullet impact and rifle noise do. Most often, the animal doesn't know anything has happened to it. It just knows it doesn't feel so good, and wanders several yards off to lie down. It dies peacefully by bleeding to death internally. A more peaceful death means the meat isn't affected by adrenalin surging through an animal's system when it's frightened or angry. Adrenalin makes the meat taste strong or "gamey" and causes it to be tough from all the lactic acid left in the muscles. The result is that people don't want to eat the meat and sometimes end up wasting it. Death by bow and arrow is more certain and peaceful than starving to death, which happens when snow depth makes moving about impossible even for the long-legged moose. The calm and quiet of meeting one's demise by bow and and arrow with a razor-sharp broadhead far outweighs the pain and terror of being pulled down and torn apart in increments by a pack of wolves or a grizzly bear. It also precludes the startled, bunching-up reaction animals have when struck by a bullet.

Waiting a half-hour or forty-five minutes before searching out the animal's final resting place assures that it won't try to struggle away when you get near it. Prudence dictates, though, that you give grizzly bears and other similarly dangerous game, like Cape buffalo or lions, more time before going to find them.

John was disillusioned with the broadheads he'd been using. In Africa, he lost a massive Cape buffalo because the broadhead on his arrow couldn't penetrate its dense bone structure. He shot five arrows in rapid succession from twenty yards, thinking that surely each would down the animal. But he had to shoot the buffalo with a rifle when it charged. And he lost a near-record grizzly at our camp in the mid 1970s. The bear brought the elbow of its foreleg back just as John released the arrow, and the broadhead bounced off leg bone instead going through the ribs to pierce the lungs. John was angry and heartbroken both times. He resolved to do something about it.

John researched and brainstormed to develop a completely unconventional prototype. The new broadhead he came up with was structured differently from those on the market. It didn't have the slim bullet or chisel tip that comes on most broadheads. Instead, he designed a heavy, bone-splitting tip patterned after those the English longbowmen in Robin Hood's time used with such deadly effect against armored opponents. Instead of three triangular blades with the bases resting in grooves in the ferrule, he designed a pair of double-sided blades that interlocked within the ferrule to create a four-blade head. But manufacturer after manufacturer spurned the idea. In spite of John's reputation as a skilled bowhunter and successful businessman, he was turned down again and again. In preretirement life, John had owned a series of restaurants in New York that did a booming business. His well-respected business acumen as a restaurateur did nothing to spark his brainchild in the broadhead trade, however. The rejections were galling. He had set out to introduce a broadhead that would produce clean kills even when it struck heavy bone. His motivation was to develop something better for bowhunters to shoot with, to assure that game didn't get away to suffer from a broadhead shot that didn't penetrate the way it should. He wasn't out to make a killing in the business sense, but when no one shared his desire for a better broadhead, he took matters into his own hands. The bowhunting industry's turning a deaf ear fired his competitive instincts.

John came out of retirement to invest a goodly amount of his savings in the venture that others ignored. The result is the Muzzy broadhead system, which bears John's high school football nickname. In building the Muzzy, he thought about all the things that were inconvenient and undependable in the other broadheads. Practice heads flew differently from hunting heads, so all the target practice was for naught in actual hunting situations. And some other broadheads were limited to either wood or aluminum arrows.

Unlike other broadheads, the Muzzy was built so practice blades would fly and weigh the same as the hunting blades, but they are dull and shaped for easy arrow removal from foam targets. Hunting tips have very hard Trocar tips to fracture bone, and the blades are Soligen German steel, the same material used for surgical tools. And the heads are readily interchangeable. He made sure the broadheads would be in components so the entire broadhead wouldn't have to be replaced if only a tip or blade got damaged. John designed the Muzzy broadheads with both glue-on and screw-on sets so they could be used on wood and aluminum arrows, and in a variety of grains, or weights, for different sizes of game.

John Musacchia was after a bull moose in the wilds of Alaska to affirm his belief in his own product. He had more invested in this hunt than just the desire to take a moose. Because he was field-testing his experimental Muzzy broadhead, his reputation as an internationally recognized bowhunter and ranking member of the Pope and Young Club was on the line. The broadhead was up against the toughest test of all: John's own exacting standards under field conditions.

I could tell John had aged since our first meeting years before: his wavy dark hair now had silver streaks, his laugh lines were a little deeper, and his pre-beard stubble showed more salt than pepper. But his sense of humor was intact and he was in good physical shape. John hunted regularly and stayed in condition by playing tennis. His massive shoulders and thick biceps were testimony to the strength needed to pull the bow to full draw and hold it there.

Pete Buist, Mike Tinker, and I were guiding John and Rambo. A perpetual-motion machine, Rambo was an intense person determined to make the most of his waking hours. While the rest of us were content to sit and use our binoculars, he was always eager to walk and find out what was beyond the next hill. He hadn't yet learned the art of patience.

This hunt began on a fall-bronzed hillside at dawn well north of the West Fork of the Gulkana River. A bull moose soon materialized in an excellent stalking location for a bowhunter, and it was large enough to be used in advertising photos. Racing about a mile uphill, we crossed through a steep, heavily willowed ravine. Then Pete, Rambo, and I sat while Tinker and Musacchia went on to complete the stalk.

"Come on ahead when you hear the shot," were the last words out of Tinker's mouth as he and John moved quickly toward the dense green alder thicket that concealed their quarry a couple hundred yards away. By the time the incongruity of his statement sank in, Tinker was too far away. I thought about whistling at his disappearing back, then decided the hell with it.

"Is Musacchia's arrow gonna break the sound barrier or what?" Pete wondered wryly as we lazed in the sun after tiring of spotting moose on far-off hillsides.

Time wore on. "D'you s'pose John has had a chance to shoot yet?" Rambo inquired. Sitting without a clue about what was going on behind that screen of brush was beginning to tell on him. He fidgeted and squirmed.

"Maybe they're gonna shoot a flaming arrow into the sky for us." I shrugged. "Tinker'll probably come charging back and tell us to hurry up, we got work to do. That's when we'll know."

One hour passed, then two. We dared not move about, not wanting to ruin John's stalk. We knew he was testing the Muzzy in hopes that it would make the cleanest, surest kill for both bowhunters and the animals they hunted.

With his development staff, he'd already done target testing, velocity readings, and puncture trials. Smaller game hunts confirmed the Muzzy's performance, but the real test was here, on big game.

If holes could be bored by staring hard with binoculars, the bushes we watched would have been Swiss cheese. At long last, I saw Tinker's head and yellow-shirted shoulders appear above the crest of the small hill. He looked exuberant and was apparently talking to himself. Without looking at us, he made a fisted gesture with both arms raised head-high, as if to say "touchdown!"

"They got 'im," I said. "Look at Tinker. He's jazzed."

Tinker was jauntily collecting the day-packs and gear he and John had left scattered on the bald, gray knoll and hadn't realized we'd been staring at him. We had already started walking when Tinker remembered us. He turned and waved. This time it was easy to see the grin on his face.

"It was beautiful," he said, meeting us halfway and breathing hard more from excitement than exertion. "We got about forty yards from that bull, and he had a bunch of cows with him that we couldn't see from the Point. I put John about sixteen or so yards out in front of me, and then I called and rattled. The cows didn't even bat an eye. They thought I was another moose. The bull kept having to round 'em back up because they came to my call. Then he decided to check out who his competition was."

I grinned at Pete and Rambo from behind Tinker, whose exhilaration was contagious. They were leaning far forward, focusing on Tinker's words, lips parted in half smiles, and facial expressions reflecting questions they wanted to ask.

Tinker chattered on, too jubilant to notice.

"John was worried. He kept looking back at me, and I motioned to him to stay put. That bull circled to get upwind of me and came right by John at twenty yards. John was great. Excellent, excellent draw. He held till the moose was real close." Tinker demonstrated with an invisible bow.

The moose didn't know what happened. He looked back where the arrow went in, then wandered back about sixty yards back into alders. Tinker and John could hear the moose breathing and recognized the sound that indicated a lung hit. They gave him about half an hour to die, then found the bull just where they expected.

John's expression spoke far more than his words. The broadhead had performed as well, better even, than he had dared to hope. Only one shot was needed to cleanly kill this bull.

Tinker and I became official photographers, plying 35-mm cameras with zoom and regular lenses. John, pleased and satisfied, was a willing subject, brandishing the Muzzy on its sylph-like arrow. Rambo, perhaps more electrified about the moose than John, kept up a running commentary.

"John, how did it feel? I mean, after you shot, did you know you had him? Hey, hold the arrow down on the moose's forehead. That oughta be a good picture. How many brochures are you gonna make?"

As we skinned and gutted the animal John sometimes looked bemused, as if afraid to believe the true potential of the product he had worked so hard to perfect.

"I don't believe it!" he would marvel. Then he would shake his head and beam again, fingering the broadhead as he talked excitedly about its future.

"My gawd, this thing is huge," Rambo reacted as he grabbed the moose's hind leg to ease my job of skinning its underside. "Do you mean to tell me you can pick one of these quarters up?"

I grinned and wiped my grimy hand against my jeaned leg. "Yep. You ought to see me stagger. If anything gets in my way before I get to the machine, I'm had. The leg lands in a pile, and I have to start over with it. I just hug the fool thing." I decided I'd better work out for the rest of my life if I expected to keep hugging hind quarters the same size as me.

"Did anybody measure the antlers?" asked John. "I got so delighted about getting this animal that I forgot about size. He's got a nice rack, though, doesn't he? Good shape, long tines."

Tinker grabbed his tape measure from his backpack and handed me one end of it. We stretched it across the expanse of antlers.

"Forty-six and three-quarters. I called it, didn't I, John?" Tinker nearly always says something like that, which makes him sound a bit of a braggart. The thing is, he rarely misses antler size by more than a quarter of an inch.

"Good size—doesn't break any Pope and Young records, but you know what? I don't care. This moose sure as hell tells me the Muzzy is the broadhead of the future."

Today, John's Muzzy brochures carry a picture of him holding the broadhead on its arrow, with the silver point resting against the dark chocolate of the moose's forehead between its antlers. The ceiling at Point Camp cabin sports, in black magic marker, John's trademark saying which graces some of our other cabin walls and ceilings:

> *Be of good cheer*
> *Muzzy was here.*

Only the rough-hewn chain-sawed spruce log wall at this cabin carries the new milestone:

> *9/13/85*
> *Friday the Thirteenth*
> *Muzzy Gets His Moose.*

One man's desire for cleaner, more humane kills has gone a long way toward better hunting. Muzzy Products has blossomed into a lucrative business that is managed by Johnny and Michelle, John and Barbara's children. The company expanded into bowfishing heads, and the Muzzy has become the top seller in several states as well as overseas.

Then in his late sixties, John had taken more than sixty big game animals by bow and arrow, nine of which are in the record books. His current hunting plans included a trip back to Alaska for a grizzly bear and another moose.

Muzzy's Pizzaiolo

3–5 pounds moose tenderloin, backstrap, or other roast, sliced into ½" thick medallions
4 Tbsp olive oil
2 Tbsp parsley
1 Tbsp each basil, oregano, black pepper
6–10 garlic cloves, diced small
2 small cans mushrooms
One 14-oz. can stewed tomatoes
One 6-oz. can tomato paste
One 8-oz. can tomato sauce
1 cup Scotch or gin
salt to taste
Sear medallions on both sides in olive oil; add garlic and saute quickly. Add stewed tomatoes, sauce and paste, mushrooms, and spices. Simmer for about an hour. Return to boil five minutes before serving; add the Scotch or gin. Serve over macaroni, cooked al dente. Can also be served over rice. For a slightly different taste, add one chopped and sauteed onion. Caribou, beef, or pork may also be substituted for the moose.

John Musacchia and the moose shot with his Muzzy broadhead and a recurve bow, 1985.

John Musacchia and the author warming by a small campfire, six miles from camp, in September 1986. Photo taken by Mike Tinker.

Red-Ass Moose

OFTEN REMINISCE ABOUT HUNTS with John Musacchia. He is an exceptionally patient hunter, and he possesses a marvelous dry wit. We would spend days roaming the hills we call the Red Knobs, combing them a few steps at a time. Stop, look, and listen. Move a few feet, stop, look, and listen. Hunting so slowly changes your focus. I always found myself relaxing, joining my surroundings instead of racing through them. Delicate leaf patterns leap out, small springs gurgle under the golden muskeg, tiny tundra and alpine flowers peek their fragile miniature heads out of the underbrush and rocks. Birds trill their morning, midday, and evening songs undisturbed for you while tawny speckled-gray grouse bob along beside you. Sometimes a curious cow moose stands twenty feet away, gazing innocently with huge, long-lashed brown eyes as you freeze midstep, waiting for her to lose interest and turn away so you can move again.

One of our day-long excursions to the Red Knobs led us near the place a bull had been when we'd spotted him from the Point, our lookout across the valley. When we finally got there a few hours later, that bull was nowhere to be seen. Instead, the area was populated with several cows and smaller bull moose. John and I had inadvertently crept into a situation that stranded us. Our search for the larger bull was blocked. We couldn't move any direction without spooking one or more of the animals. We didn't want to do that because they would alert the larger bull that trouble was brewing. So we stood, John's brown leather and tweed hat and my short red mop of hair absorbing the warm afternoon sun.

We whispered back and forth, shifting from leg to leg and looking warily around. The moose ambled with seeming aimlessness from bush to bush, long pink tongues wrapping around the willow and alder tops and pulling the leaves off to munch. They slipped so easily through the tangled brush that constantly caught our feet and caused us to stumble.

After an hour or so of being held captive by the meandering moose, we decided to blow the stalk. Both of us were fidgety, dusk would soon be falling, and no larger moose had appeared while we waited.

"Might as well go," John muttered. "If we're lucky, maybe we can get outta here without spookin' 'em too bad."

101

"Okay. If you don't trip and fall, I won't either," I said with a grin. John made a face and stuck his tongue out at me. Earlier each of us had taken a spill in the twisted branch understructure of the frosted dwarf birch that covered the hillsides in deep burgundy and orange shades of red. We had laughed at the other's misfortune. I knew John detested these bushes. I'd heard him refer to the dwarf birch as "the souls of the damned reaching up from Hell to grab at your ankles, yelling 'Save me, save me.'"

We turned and eased away to the east, directly through a shoulder-high field of the fiendish dwarf birch. John, in the lead, carried his bow with the string side up, centered on his head. He was practicing what we knew—that sometimes moose won't spook and run if they see a headdress that looks similar to a set of antlers in the right place on a body.

A little way along, I heard John snicker. Then he stopped and turned, red-faced from choked-back laughter.

"What's so funny?" I asked quizzically, puzzled but grinning in response to his infectious muffled snorts.

"These poor animals have never seen a moose with a red ass before!" He doubled over in more smothered snorts.

"Huh?" I frowned, unable to follow his drift.

John regained his composure.

"Think about it. I got this ridiculous bow on my head, you and your red head are following me. Now what the hell does a moose see from behind us? A moose with a red ass! They must be so damn confused!" He put the bow back on his head, swung his hips and minced a few steps. And went off into another fit of stifled laughter. The picture he painted tickled my funny-bone. We laughed until we were weak-kneed. Muted paroxysms of giggles plagued us as we followed the twisting, turning game trails back to camp.

Can We Call a Bigger Tractor?

STUCK WAS AN UNDERSTATEMENT. Four hours were gone, and we were just as bogged down as when we started. I stopped my whirling-dervish of shoveling to step back and survey the debacle. Wayne's diesel Bombardier was hopelessly mired in a silty, quicksand-like creek, gripped by the thick muck that was hidden under the thin grey mud oozing past the slowly submerging engine. The pintle-hitched trailer rested askew off to one side where we had unceremoniously left it. Moose pieces and gear littered the celery-green muskeg tussocks behind us; in front of me, spruce trees and branches stuck out at crazy angles from under the Bombardier's tracks. I stood on one of the rear sideboards, while the front of the Bombardier pointed nearly skyward. Typically, the sideboards on the back of the machine are my shoulder height—about five feet off the ground.

The day had started innocently enough. Ted and Norbert and Tinker and I had slept in a little after Norbert's successful moose hunt the previous day. A couple days earlier, we'd happened on this spot—a nice flat area about a hundred yards from a lake—and had set up camp.

"Setting up camp" meant tying tarps from the top of the Bombardier to adjacent brush, forming an open-sided tent with a roof of sorts to shield the cots we slept on from rain. It also meant setting the wood stove out in the open where its galvanized chimney, proudly erect with no roof to go through, puffed warm spruce smoke into the sky. The brown kitchen table with its removable pipe-threaded legs (made by Dale Ruth) stood near the wood stove, while the metal food boxes doubled as chairs, since we had four people and only two folding chairs.

We had awakened to a clear day, completely different from the grey mist of the morning before, so thick that anything twenty feet away was lost. Although we'd had to wait until afternoon before the fog lifted enough to hunt, Norbert collected his trophy. Before he did, I was treated to an awe-inspiring display of bull moose dominance when Norbert's bull hooked a cow under her belly with his antlers and tossed her in the air. This day, we speedily cooked breakfast and broke camp quickly. Ted's moose was still in the trailer, and we were going to add

103

Norbert's trophy to the load before setting a course for Island Lake where Wayne was to meet us the next day. He was also bringing Aisha, Tinker's daughter, who would join us for the last few days of the season.

We finally left around noon—later than the 9:00 a.m. departure originally planned, even though there were no tents to break down, since we'd been living gypsy style. Island Lake was only a four-hour trip, so there was no need to worry about time. Tinker decided to take a direct line to Norbert's moose, rather than follow the trail. We ground merrily along, the Bombardier climbing over downed trees with the trailer following dutifully, the composite rig looking like an articulated dinosaur.

Lulled by the peace of the day and the ease with which the machine toiled along, we slacked off on our watch for potential potholes. We chugged between a couple of large spruce trees, wiggled to the left, crawled over a tussock and began our way across a velvety green expanse, headed toward a small incline that was encumbered by a newly fallen large spruce tree. I felt the Bombardier's churning forward momentum turn sickeningly sluggish.

I snapped to attention; Tinker also reacted immediately, stomping on the accelerator. The Bombardier responded, charging across the lawn-like expanse as the green moss gave way to suctioning mud and water beneath. Instead of muskeg growing on firm tundra, we had wandered onto a thinly covered, silt-laden creek. I relaxed a little as the Bombardier began to crawl up on the fallen tree, just as it had done with several others between the camp and here. Up and over the log, and we would be home free. This time, though, the machine slid back. Tinker tried again, with the same result.

He tried to back up, but the trailer jack-knifed against a tussock we had just trundled over. The back of the Bombardier's tracks began to dig in and the trailer started to sink. We frantically tossed moose pieces and gear out of the trailer and disconnected it from the Bombardier. Struggling, the four of us finally muscled it aside.

Tinker tried to back up once more, to no avail. The Bombardier only sank deeper, grey ooze dripping from the tracks as they spun in the muck.

We were confident of a quick escape, though, because we had a winch on the back of the machine. We rolled the cable out, wrapped it around the only big fat spruce tree at the rear of the machine, and engaged the gears. With the pull from the winch, the Bombardier moved a bit and the suction on the tracks began to release.

Then I heard a metallic "ping" and the winch stopped. I felt a jolt in the pit of my stomach. The U-joint on the power take-off had broken. Rendered helpless by the unanticipated mechanical failure, the four of us stood and stared. The woods seemed unusually silent.

A five-hour stuck in the Alphabet Hills in 1993.

"Is anybody nearby?" Norbert asked. "When this happens at home (Ted and Norbert are farmers from Iowa), we just call the nearest neighbor with a bigger tractor."

Tinker and I exchanged a glance. No neighbors here, and even if other hunters were somewhere in the area, we would never know it.

"Will the radio work? Maybe somebody can hear us if we call for help." Ted was ever the optimist.

"Well, the radio works," Tinker replied, "but the only person that could hear us would be Wayne if he happened to fly over, and we don't expect him until evening. Even then, he'd look for us on the trail, closer to Island Lake. We're just gonna have to figure out a way to get this thing out of here."

"Could Wayne drop us an extra chain?" Ted wondered.

"Not likely," Tinker replied, "since he won't even be looking for us."

The men grabbed axes, the chain saw, and the come-along, and I grabbed shovels. While they cut small spruce trees and trimmed the large branches off the downed spruce that had stymied the Bombardier, I concentrated on keeping the muck moving past the engine.

I had two shovels, one a long-handled Number 2 (with a rounded point for digging soft dirt), and the other a sawed-off Number 1 (a square-edged blade best known to Alaskans for its snow removal capability). I alternated between the two, because neither one worked particularly well for directing the flow of the watery silt. Sometimes I shoveled great gobs of the goo away, and sometimes I just used the shovel like a large spatula, pushing the quaggy mass past the engine.

If the engine quit while part of it was under the water and muck, the Bombardier would probably not start again. If that happened, the whole shooting-match might disappear into the muck. I knew others who had lost their equipment just that way.

If the machine sank, about two hundred thousand dollars worth of machinery, camp gear, and personal gear would become forest filler. And we would be semi-stranded. Walking to the Denali Highway or to Island Lake was possible, but neither would be fun. Going north to the Denali would probably be a three-day hike with the hunters—and we would have the Middle Fork of the Gulkana River to contend with. Island Lake would take a day for Tinker and me, maybe two with the hunters.

And the moose. To permanently leave it would mean breaking the law. We would have to somehow go back to retrieve it, or face the consequences of wantonly wasting game.

Those thoughts spurred me to lean my whole anxiety-driven body into my task, stopping every now and again to add my strength to the pulling power of the come-along.

Ted and Norbert ran the chain saw to get trees, and scurried back to the machine with them. They were using a universal method of getting unstuck: stuffing trees and sticks and branches under the tracks, in hopes that the debris would bottom out, or at least give enough stability so the tracks would catch and allow the machine to crawl out. But the trees silently disappeared into the bottomless goo and the tracks continued to turn and the machine didn't move anywhere except farther down into the muck.

When the Bombardier's tracks spun in Tinker's efforts to get the machine out, they reminded me of a piece of fur that undulates when you stroke it. The bottom of the circular track arched up to meet its top, stopping when it bumped up against the bogie wheels which are part of the running gear.

As soon as my come-along help was over, I'd return to the shoveling. My back was on fire, and my arms felt alternately like spaghetti and knotted ropes. My blue Chena River Run T-shirt was soaked with sweat, and nearly all of me was coated with the wet silty muck. Work like this toughens up a person's hands. At the beginning of the season, I can easily feel my soft contact lenses; at the end of the season, I have to look to see if the lens is even on my finger-tip.

I prayed for the nightmare to end, and feared that it wouldn't—or if it did, the outcome would be all wrong.

After about six hours of not gaining a particle of forward movement, Tinker had what I call a "lightbulb." He jumped out of the Bombardier and hollered at me, "Get me the chains and the handyman jack!"

I reached down into the bed of the Bombardier and pulled out the two long, stout chains we carried with us. I slogged through the muck with them to the front of the machine, where Ted or Norbert had already taken the handyman jack.

"What are you going to do?" I asked.

"If you take the handle off the jack and put it on upside-down, you turn the jack into a giant come-along! If we have enough chain to reach that big spruce up there in front of us, we might have enough leverage to pull ourselves out. If the tracks can get purchase on anything, we'll be out of this hole in no time."

Tinker moved quickly as he spoke, reversing the handle and sending us to hook the chain they'd been using with the come-along onto the front of the Bombardier. The other chain went from the slotted end of the jack to the tree and was wrapped around it.

It was going to take Ted, Norbert, and me to reef on the handyman jack handle, two pulling and one pushing, since we'd be trying to move about 8,000 pounds of Bombardier.

"Jeez, you guys," I said to Ted and Norbert, "we better look out. If a chain snaps with all that tension on it, we'll be dead ducks." Their faces pale and solemn, they nodded. All of us knew that there was no way to get to a hospital if anyone got seriously injured. Since there was no other way to get out, though, we all hunkered into our task. Tinker manned the driver's seat, ready to use the machine's power to help us while we worked the jack handle.

Ever so slowly, the jack handle ratcheted to its limit. We brought it back, ratcheted it down again, repeating the process over and over. We looked over our shoulders, expecting the tree that was our deadman to uproot and tumble over on us. Its root structure quaked and swayed under the unstable muskeg, but held firm. Twice we had to completely reconnect the chains because the Bombardier inched so close to the jack that we couldn't ratchet any more. Finally, the machine came free. We unhooked the jack and the chains, and watched in a wave of relief as the Bombardier scuttled away from the hole.

Tinker circled around, avoiding the mossy expanse. Rather than backing up to the trailer, because it would mean going back to the hell-hole we had just gotten out of, we stretched one of our trusty chains out to the trailer. Using the machine, we tugged it around so it was aiming the right direction, and then pulled it up over the tussock it had jack-knifed against. After reloading the trailer with the moose and gear, we sat down to refuel ourselves with food and water. Ted looked at me and laughed.

"You oughtta see yourself," he hooted. "The only clean spot is your left shoulder!" The others joined his hilarity. One glance at my T-shirt and pants and so did I. I had obviously used all of my body when I was shoveling the silt past the Bombardier's engine. The men were dirty on only the bottom half. The laughter turned out to be a good tension-reliever. We all relaxed, feeling giddy now that we had overcome the danger.

About twenty minutes later, we had picked up Norbert's moose and returned to the trail. Strangely, nobody mentioned taking a shortcut this time. Trail running would get us to Island Lake after dark, but so what? We had headlights. Besides, if Wayne came over, he would see us.

Once again, we thought we were home free. I was thinking of a sponge bath at Island Lake and of warm, clean, dry clothes. Dinner plans danced in my head as I reviewed possible meals for the evening. Ted and Norbert looked relaxed, and seemed to be relishing the thought that the end of their hunt was finally near.

Except that suddenly the Bombardier felt sluggish again. I frowned. We were on a good, solid trail, so there shouldn't have been any reason for the machine to balk.

"Sharon, walk alongside. See if there's a tree caught in the tracks or something," Tinker commanded.

So I hopped out from my post in the back and trotted along, first in front of the machine to look for large sticks and small trees that might be hanging up in the tracks. Next I walked on the right side, then on the left, bent over for a better view of what might be amiss. Nothing wrong there. I waited for the trailer to go by. The left side was fine, but the trailer bed looked crooked. When I went around to the right side, the problem became immediately obvious. The trailer body was riding hard against its large airplane tire, and it had been that way long enough to peel a groove about an inch deep in the hard rubber.

"Tinker, stop!" I hollered, as I ran to catch up with the Bombardier. "The trailer box is cattywampus. It's cutting into the tire."

We discovered that we had been losing the leaf springs. The long, curved pieces of iron that gave suspension to the trailer were nearly gone, and the support members that held the trailer box in place were loose and crooked.

We backtracked a little on foot but didn't find any of the missing springs. Since dark was rapidly approaching, we pulled out the rest of the loose springs, and replaced them with wedges we manufactured out of some small green spruce trees. We again moved along toward Island Lake, this time very slowly.

Still in wet, muddy clothes, I had gotten chilled. Since it was obvious that Island Lake was probably still three hours away at our current snail's pace, we decided to find a level spot along the trail to spend the night. Fumbling in the dark, we got tarps stretched out, cots and sleeping bags set up, and the Coleman stove going. With Dinty Moore beef stew heating in its own can and the coffee warming, I ducked behind a bush to change into dry clothes. The men disappeared to their own changing bushes, and soon we were all around the Coleman lantern, steaming bowls and cups in hand.

We fell onto the cots, exhausted. I vowed silently to make sure weightlifting was a winter-long activity. If I hadn't stayed in good shape, I'd have been hurting even worse now. Come morning, no one was eager to move. Finally, coaxing aching bodies out of our sleeping bags, through breakfast, and into the Bombardier, we were on our way.

No more mishaps befell us, and we reached Island Lake in the early afternoon. Wayne and Aisha had been waiting for us since around noon of "stuck day"—about twenty-four hours, in all. It felt like a week to me.

"What's been keeping you?" Wayne took one look at the silt still coated on the Bombardier, and the leaf springs sticking out of the trailer and continued with a grin, "Have a few problems, did you?"

The four of us soon had him updated on the happenings of the last day. He laughed, having experienced similar mishaps during the years that he and his brother Mel had operated almost solely with Bombardiers. He seemed almost wistful, as though he had missed out on the fun. Then it was back to business—he had moose and people to fly out.

I still have the blue shirt that I wore that day. It faintly shows the infamous mudline. The clean part—the left sleeve and shoulder, from armpit to neckline—remains a little brighter than the rest of the mud-dimmed shirt.

Weasel Antics

T HE LITTLE WEASEL HESITANTLY reached its paw out, craned its neck to look up at me, then stretched to touch the toe of my boot. Tap, tap. I couldn't feel the gentle touch through my tough leather boots, of course, but I could sense the quivering curiosity that had overcome this pint-sized creature, making it brave enough to come so close. I stared down without moving a muscle, barely breathing, as the face atop the tiny brown, sinuous body peered up at me. The weasel was poised to flee at my slightest movement. After a few seconds that stretched into an eternity, it reached out for another touch, and then sniffed the boot's toe before flipping over backwards and leap-scampering into the brush.

Our brown-topped, cream-tummied little friend was a least weasel, part of the Mustelidae family, which includes mink, marten, river and sea otter, and wolverine. Its counterpart is the short-tailed weasel, a larger version that grows to about fifteen inches long in comparison to the ten-inch length of the least weasel. Since both are top-notch mousers, they are excellent camp neighbors. In fact, because they have such a high metabolic rate, weasels need to eat roughly half their weight every day.

The weasel had appeared on our spotting point during moose season's second day. Evidently its home was somewhere nearby on our hillside, for it visited us daily for over a week, rustling through the dwarf birch as it raced from one to another of us for a quick peek before dashing away again. Weasels are a constant blur of motion, and this one was so fast it seemed to be making up for lost time. It also looked like a juvenile; instead of being ten inches long, it was more like six or seven inches. It appeared to be concerned about these large invaders of its hillside as it ran back and forth along its maze of paths, checking us out.

Our hunters didn't have the patience to be still long enough to see what the curious little creature would do. They did, however, discover that the weasel didn't care one whit for peanut butter and not much more for cheese. Sausage or lunch meat, though, was a different story. It would pluck the meat out from between the buttered, mustardy remains of a sandwich, race fifteen feet or so, gobble a bite, and disappear with the remainder. We never found where it was stashing the food we didn't see it eat.

My husband Michael and I often stayed at the Point after the hunters retired to the cabin. The season hadn't been a good one for moose—the weather was warm and the hunters were noisy—so I was squeezing every ounce of glassing out of the daylight each day in the hopes that I'd spot an evening moose for a next morning stalk. After the hunters headed for camp, Michael and I would pick up the two-foot by three-foot sections of Ensolite pad that served as sitting cushions while we were glassing. We piled them under the blue tarp tied off to a nearby spruce tree. Rocks held the pads in place so the wind wouldn't waft them away, but the weight didn't prevent the pads from curling at each end.

Our little weasel was entranced with the pads. It considered them its private gymnastics room and treated us to a captivating nightly exhibition. I forgot to look for moose, and we often had to head for the cabin in almost total dark. The weasel ran inside the pads, through the upside down curves, did a backflip, and leaped to the next level of pads. There it did push-ups of its own creation. It stood on its hind legs, reached tall with its tiny front paws and pushed, pushed, pushed to make the pads bounce up and down. Then it'd repeat the circuit, flipping, turning, and rolling as it went. The weasel would pop out from the pads, peer at us, and dive back in. Sometimes a little squeak would accompany its departure.

Each day, the weasel's inquisitive face told us that it was curious about us. Michael and I decided to be as still as we could; we would wait and see if our entertaining little friend would overcome its apprehension about us—and if it

Inquisitive weasel, September 1997. Photo by Helmut Ringelstein.

did, what it would do. Each evening the weasel would come a little closer, then run from side to side in front of us as we stood stock-still. It would sit up on short hind legs for a quick second, pop down, and run the other direction. Finally, at long last, it screwed up its courage and advanced.

Then came the night it touched my boot. It seemed to lose its fear—and some elements of its curiosity—after that. The next evening it didn't appear as quickly as before, and we began to think that perhaps it had departed. But it came back again. This time the weasel was more direct. It played in the pads for a while, before charging straight over to us. It investigated both of my boots, ran between my feet and inspected me all around. Then it moved on to Michael and continued its scrutiny. Finally it sat up, chittered at us, and disappeared.

This little character wasn't the only weasel around. At the cabin, an adult short-tailed weasel had adopted a hole in the ground and excavated a home for itself. Late in the evening we could hear it rustling in the plastic garbage bag outside the cabin. I believe the weasel, promptly dubbed "Herman the Ermine," thought that bag was a gold mine for all the noise it made scrounging through our leftovers.

One day we discovered Herman was appropriating meat scraps from trimmed moose. We were sitting outside in the pale sunshine eating lunch, when a long strip of dried meat sprang to life. It seemed to be scooting across the ground of its own accord. Then we noticed Herman tugging the strip through the fallen leaves as it hopped backwards. When it reached its hole, it would try to go down headfirst, which didn't work because it and the piece of meat wouldn't fit through the hole together. Finally, Herman disappeared into the hole headfirst, turned around and popped back out to grab the strip and pull it in. As the weasel was commandeering its third strip of meat, Pete Buist, a member of our guide crew, decided to have a little fun. When Herman dove into the hole on the third trip, Pete stretched his tall frame out until he was flat on his stomach, grabbed the end of the meat and held on as the weasel tugged, and tugged again. Pete answered with duplicate tugs. Soon, the weasel got suspicious. It popped its head out of the hole, saw Pete's bearded face an arm's length away, shrieked, and dove back into the hole. We dissolved into laughter—I think Pete was as startled as that short-tailed weasel.

Later, the inquisitive little creature grew brave enough to come on the porch and accept hand-held morsels of raw meat. And no one thought to take a picture.

Camp Robber Lushes

G RAY JAYS, COMMONLY KNOWN to most Alaskans as camp robbers, are noisy scavengers. They seem to know within minutes of your arrival that you're at camp for the season and will be cooking food. You find them perched on spruce trees right outside the tent or cabin in hopes that you'll toss a scrap out. They squawk and chatter and fly/hop from branch to branch. They try to commandeer any food that you might set down for just a moment, and I've even had them land on the edge of the outdoor washbasin when I was washing my hair.

Somehow, their divining systems are even more finely tuned to when a moose is down. As you toss away pieces of fat when you're skinning the moose, camp robbers squabble over it almost before it hits the ground. Opportunists that they are, they follow you back to camp, continuing to peck at the moose after you've got it on the meatpole. I run at them and throw sticks, especially when they peck at the tenderloins.

For all the aggravation they can cause, they are a part of nature's circle. Their squabbling over food alerts other animals to the potential for a free meal. If people, especially hunters, are alert to what camp robbers are up to, they can discover a bear-cached kill or an animal killed by wolves. If you're a guide and have a bear hunter, being aware of camp robbers' habits can lead you to a dead animal. Keeping an eye on it could result in a bear to hunt, if the bear pays attention to the same signals.

One year, some of our hunters decided to see what camp robbers would do with left-over pancakes. They tore the pancakes into inch-square pieces and amused themselves by holding the pieces until the camp robbers got brave enough to fly up and snatch the pancake shreds from their hand. Then the men came up with the idea of soaking the pancakes in the last of the Jack Daniels. They laid the soaked pieces on the table, on top of empty V-8 cans, and on tree branches—anywhere to test the camp robbers' agility. The birds must have loved the flavor, because they flocked back faster and faster. Trouble was, their landings became less and less sure—they would miss the table or the tree branch. The more they ate, the funnier they got. Several camp robbers smacked into the washpan and plopped onto the table. They wobbled on willow branches; their squawks slurred. They teetered upon take-off, their ordinarily sure flight tilting at crazy angles. The birds had us in stitches.

We worried about them, though. How much Jack Daniels can a bird stand? What about bird hangovers and headaches? Do they have a bush remedy we humans don't know about? I knew they ate fermented blueberries and cranberries, and in town, gobbled yeasty chokecherries, passing out on lawns in a stupor. After a while, as though they'd slept off their inebriation, they would fly away, seeming none the worse for the wear.

We knew that some of the pancake and Jack Daniels scavengers survived unscathed and surmised that the rest had also. There were a few camp robbers with distinctive characteristics—one was missing all the claws on one foot, another had a broken wing, and a third was missing some feathers on the top of its head. Those three and hordes of others were back that evening and each day after that.

If only they could tell us what they thought—and felt!

A camprobber or gray jay being hand-fed a piece of pancake.

Wolves

THE WOLVES THAT FREQUENTLY serenade us at night are highly social animals. They live in packs that range from six to sometimes as many as thirty animals, in any combination of parents, pups, yearlings, and other adults. The wolves we've seen are usually well-mixed shades of gray and tan. Although at first glance they can look like a dog, a second glance shows you their long, slender legs topped by an equally rangy body that looks out of proportion. A dog seems to be a more compact unit because its legs are shorter than its body is long, while the wolf is the opposite. Wolves also look scruffier. There is a social order within each pack, with separate dominance hierarchies for males and females.

Their vocalization is what most people are familiar with. Their crescendoing howls start low and undulate up and down the scale, sometimes rising to a yip and then ending abruptly. Sometimes the wolves will howl for only a few minutes. Some nights, though, they sing for the better part of an hour, and it sounds like they move from place to place. Of course, there could be wolves in different locations talking to each other. The howls, which often sound lonely and plaintive to us, are their way of communicating with each other. I frequently wonder what they're talking about when they sing their long or short conversations.

Although we hear them a lot at night, it's not often we see them during the day. We do, though, see the results of their hunting.

Once, when we stopped the Bombardier so Tinker could pull debris from the tracks to make steering easier, I walked ahead to do some glassing. You never know when a moose will show itself, and we had a hunter with us. I stopped at the crest of a small hill to search the long valley in front of me. When the Bombardier growled up, I went over to crawl in, only to meet Tinker crawling out.

"What's up?" I asked, puzzled. Tinker was moving with a purpose.

"Didn't you see the caribou?"

"What caribou?"

Just below where I'd been standing, in a depression hidden from me by the dwarf birch, was a dead young caribou with its soft underbelly slashed open in several places. Its guts trailed behind. It was easy to see by the varied stages of

Roberta (left), Sharon (middle), and Myrtle McLeod with a black wolf that turned out to be rabid. Buzzy remains watchful in the background.

A wolf track with a 30.06 shell for size: Johnson River, 1991.

dried and clotted blood that it had slowly bled to death; the bushes where its legs had thrashed were bent and broken.

That particular caribou was cold and the morning sun was still melting frost from its hide; others we've stumbled across were more recently killed—not cold yet, but stiffening. Finding a still-warm caribou with its guts hanging out is grim evidence that wolves don't always hunt to eat—especially when you go back a few days later and the carcass is the same, except for birds picking at it.

Wolves don't concentrate just on animals that can't bite back. One season not long ago, Pete Buist, Tinker, a couple of hunters, and I watched a pack of six wolves playfully chase a grizzly bear for the better part of an hour. Through the spotting scope, we could see their tongues lolling out and their tails wagging. It seemed that they were more intent on harassing the bear than killing it. The grizzly spun in its plagued travel every now and then to lunge at a wolf, swatting with a powerful forepaw. It became so irritated at the wolves diving in, nipping at its heels that every so often it sat on its rear end and whaled away with its front legs. Occasionally, the bear would connect. A wolf would fly end over end through the air to land with a thump. Each clobbered wolf looked as though the wind was knocked out of it, because it would lie still for a moment or two, then get up and stagger out of range. Soon it would rejoin the fray, limping. Eventually, the sun glinting on their fur, the bear and its tormentors disappeared from view.

Pete, Tinker, and I added up the years of outdoor experience among the three of us, and came up with just over a hundred years. None of us had ever seen wolves tormenting a grizzly. That year, though, there were also reports of wolves killing a grizzly in Denali National Park. The wolves either were braver or chasing bears was a more common activity than we knew.

The wolves we saw beleaguering the grizzly were the first I'd ever encountered when we were hunting; the only other ones I'd seen were during the fifties around our homestead. My experiences cement my belief—and confirms the statement of many others—that there are a great many wolves in the wild that humans never see.

Occasionally, all you see are tracks that tell a story . . . but only part of a story. Two years running, we saw the tracks of a grizzly, and following that grizzly, stepping in its tracks, was a large lone wolf. I surmised, rightly or wrongly, that the loner was old and no longer had a pack, and it knew that by following the grizzly it could finagle whatever the bear didn't eat, scrounging while the bear was gone.

Turbulence

I N THE LATE 1980s AND early 1990s, hunting and guiding in Alaska experienced many changes. By fall 1990, subsistence issues played a large role in altering drawing and permit hunts and shortening hunting seasons; heavy winter snows and record cold temperatures also took a toll on moose populations.

By early summer, we knew our moose season was going to be only ten rather than the usual twenty days. We canceled roughly half our guide contracts, refunding money to clients. Then in late July the other shoe dropped, hard. The moose season shrank to five days, with the new wrinkle that nonresidents were not allowed to hunt. All our contracts with nonresident hunters had to be canceled. Fortunately, none of the hunters had purchased airline tickets. I don't know what we would have done if they had.

Instead of the normal September 1–20 season, this one was to begin on September 5 and run through September 9. That gave Alaska residents five full days to hunt for a moose. And not just any bull moose would do; the area we hunt then had a minimum thirty-six inch antler size rule (now, it's fifty inches) or three brow tines. Also, today it's possible to shoot a spike-fork moose and be legal.

"What are we going to do?" I asked Wayne and Tinker in mid-August. Earlier in the year Wayne, owner of the diesel Bombardier and the airplane and original holder of the once restricted guide area, was so disillusioned that he had almost decided not to guide. He was thinking about hunting for himself instead. Now the decision was made for all three of us. Tinker's and Wayne's responses were identical: insurance was too expensive for only five days worth of resident drop-off hunters.

"Maybe we'll go hunt for ourselves for a change, and see if Wanie and Babe want to go along to help with expenses. At least that'll give 'em an opportunity to hunt. They both want to go," Wayne added.

Don Wanie from Juneau and Babe Evans from Anchorage were regular drop-off hunters and good friends as well. Tinker already planned to take Don Cameron, a neighbor, in return for hauling the gas Bombardier on his new flatbed truck. Tinker knew two other neighbors who would be happy to go along, sharing expenses for the chance to hunt. We agreed to meet at Tangle Lakes on September 3, Wayne arriving from Willow with the diesel Bombardier and Tinker coming from Fairbanks with the gas version. I would drive Tinker's three-quarter-ton Ford pickup with the extra barrels of fuel and anything else that wouldn't fit in the Bombardier and flatbed truck.

On September 2, normally the second day of hunting, a stomach flu bug flattened me, a fitting beginning to an already chaotic moose season. I was supposed to be all packed to drive to Tangle Lakes so our crew could leave with the two Bombardiers on the fourth, and instead I was immobilized.

I still had to pack my gear, turning it from a mountain on the floor into a neatly stuffed duffel bag. Luckily all the grocery shopping was done and I had my grizzly bear tag. The phone rang.

"Well, Red, are ya all packed and ready to roll? I can come over now to get the food. I can load it in the Bombardier now and we won't have to do it at Tangles!" Tinker's effervescent voice burbled into my ear.

"Hi, Tinker."

"Boy, you sound rotten. Are you okay?" Tinker was about as subtle as a sledge hammer. He agreed to come pick up the food, and I managed to convince him that I'd be ready to go tomorrow.

When the flu lasted only ten hours, I decided the hunting gods still liked me. I tottered around the house, packing and making sure my precious pressure cookers were in the "go" pile. They speed the cooking process and with their locking lids, they transform any meal into an instantly portable one for a Bombardier field trip. Plus, bears can bat them around without getting at the food in them.

The next day dawned gloomily, pouring rain. By noon it slowed to an intermittent drizzle, so Michael and I packed the pickup and drove off to sight in my rifles. I thought my 30.06 would be just fine, but I hadn't yet shot the .416 Remington.

The .416 was a combined anniversary, birthday, and Christmas present from Michael. He worried about me every year, knowing how frequently we had grizzlies in camp. When Remington began to manufacture the .416's, he waited until Tinker had his and it proved to be a good bear gun, then surreptitiously ordered one for me. I was delighted. It was my heart's desire, but I couldn't justify the expense. Michael could, though; he knows how to keep me happy—and safe.

I was right about the 30.06. At 150 yards, it fired in the seven, eight, and bulls-eye rings of the smallbore rifle fifty-yard target. That was good enough for any moose. Then we tried the .416 (I call it "Baby Bazooka")—but at $3.00 per shell, we didn't blast away with abandon. At a hundred yards the hole it blew made the 30.06 look like a .22. It was accurate. Besides, chances were that I'd never take a long shot with it. Looking for a wounded bear means that any shot you're likely to get will be twenty-five yards or less.

Everyone was already at Tangle Lakes, except for Tinker and Don Cameron. I parked next to the cabin and saw a head inside pop up in the window. Somebody alerted the rest of the crew that I was there.

Arriving at Tangles is always full of hugs and teasing, then putting the coffee pot on. Wayne, blue eyes twinkling, hopped out of his chair to give me a hug. Curly-haired, cheerful Don Wanie and ebullient Babe were right behind him. Wayne's big eight-year-old German shepherd, Sam, my buddy since he was a pup, jumped up and placed his paws on my shoulders, slurping my face with his long, floppy tongue. Bob Anconetoni and Peggy Raybeck hung back—I knew Peggy because she, Tinker, and I all work for the same agency, but I had only heard of Bob. They were Tinker's neighbors in Ester, a Fairbanks "suburb."

Tinker and Don Cameron arrived about eight o'clock, amid more hugs and bantering. Then we settled down to a mouth-watering dinner of Italian-sausage and red wine spaghetti that Don Wanie's wife, Mary, had prepared and sent along with him. We went to bed early, listening to rain pounding on the roof, hoping it would let up by morning.

By morning's gray light, I had already been wished several "Happy Birthdays," breakfast was finished, and we were outside doing last-minute packing and fueling. The rain stopped, allowing us to work fast enough to hit the trail for our thirty-mile trip by seven o'clock.

I was driving the gas Bombardier for the first time ever. My birthday, in an ordinary year, is the fourth day of hunting, and I would be found sitting on a fall-foliaged hillside, one ear tuned for the hum of Wayne and his Cessna 172 coming to airdrop my annual birthday cake. In a normal hunting season, Wayne flew and I drove his diesel machine.

At the beginning of most seasons when Wayne and I drove to the trailhead and he took the flatbed back to Tangles, he would tell me to wait until he drove away before I took off down the trail. He and his brother Mel used to drive hunters back and forth in the Bombardiers before they learned to fly, and he dearly loves the overland trip. When he flies out to spend a few days guiding and hunting, it's tacitly understood that he takes command of the machine. I knew it tortured him to have to stay behind, and I always felt terrible for the first hour or so. If it had been in my power to have him magically be in two places at once, I would have done it.

This year, though, we were all infantry, and he drove his own machine. I enjoyed watching him. Two things told me he was having a marvelous time tooling around in the Bombardier: the expression on his face and his extra, solicitous fiddling with the machine whenever our little caravan stopped. It had been at least eleven years since he'd had the opportunity to make the trip by land instead of by air. Flying responsibilities kept him so busy, he hadn't even been able to guide or to hunt for himself.

We dressed in rain gear, expecting the worst from Mother Nature. She fooled us, though, and by the time we reached the Middle Fork of the Gulkana River, we had all stripped down to our regular coats. The weather was behaving and both channels of the Middle Fork crossing were normal, the water only a foot and one-half deep. We stopped for lunch and to refuel the machines, then set out across the flats for the steep half-mile climb leading us to the mountain passes that would take us to our respective hunting grounds.

The steep climb was uneventful, quite a switch from the year before. This year, we tooled straight up the regular trail without a pause. I was standing in the back with Bob and Peggy, who had never ridden in a Bombardier. They were in awe of its performance and its ability to negotiate the seemingly insurmountable hill. I grinned wryly, thinking they should have seen last year.

Then, the spring and summer had been so dry that the gravel and dirt on the well-used trail acted like a sea of marbles, causing the Bombardier's tracks to spin in place and send us sliding backwards and sideways. Leaving the Bombardier in gear made it free-wheel, going much faster than you wanted, so you had to be quick: let off the gas with your right foot while pushing in the clutch with your left, and simultaneously pull both steering levers to brake. As soon as your right foot is free, mash it on the brake pedal to help out the braking action of the steering levers. It took more than five tries for each Bombardier to get up the hill. We had to back down each time, pushing the balloon-tired trailer hooked with a pintle hitch that was hard to steer in reverse even under perfect conditions.

With very little room to maneuver, we had to get off the bare trail into the brush where the tracks could gain some purchase. I waited until I thought Tinker, who was ahead of me, was far enough up not to roll back and hit me in case he had trouble, then started up.

My heart lodged at the back of my tongue and stayed there. All I could think about was sliding sideways on the steep slope and rolling the machine, ruining one hundred thousand dollars worth of Bombardier and an untold amount of equipment and food, not to mention squashing us. With hot and icy-cold prickly fear crawling up my spine into my scalp, I managed to work the Bombardier into the brush, where the branches and muskeg gave better traction. We slowly crept to the top of the grade with only a few more nerve-wracking slips.

Tinker, Don Cameron, Bob, Peggy, and I were in one machine, while Wayne, Don Wanie, Babe, and Sam were in the second Bombardier. We parted company about an hour past the top of the hill. They turned left toward Twin Lakes en route to Achin' Back, where they planned to hunt. We turned right, headed for Point Camp.

"See you in a few days," Wayne yelled as the others waved.

"Okay," we hollered back. "Good luck!"

They planned to hunt gypsy-style, spike camping as they worked their way along the fifteen miles farther from Achin' Back to Point Camp.

We left Bob and Peggy at a cabin on a clear, fast-moving creek loaded with grayling. They would hunt here until we returned. With a last wave, we forged on toward Point Camp, arriving just before dark. We carried the first armload of gear to the cabin, grabbed the claw hammer from its resting place on a nail pounded into the logs, and pulled out the spikes that held the door shut and, we hoped, safe from a grizzly bear's curiosity.

"Tinker," I said as I peered around the interior of the cabin, "look, no squirrels got in this time."

"No," came his muffled reply from somewhere outside, "but we've got a God-damned porcupine under the cabin."

I went out. We kicked the left-over roofing tin stacked at the back of the cabin, rattled pans, and beat on the floor, but to no avail. The fat porcupine only blinked. At least it hadn't chewed its way into the cabin. Not only are they messy, they stink nearly as badly as a skunk. I've had to clean up after one only once, a still-vivid memory.

By dinnertime the rain had begun again, and by bedtime it poured in earnest. Don's roaring fire in the wood stove warmed the comfortable log cabin. We were all cozy in our sleeping bags.

"Hope this stops, or at least slows down, by morning. I don't want to hunt in the rain," Tinker said. After a pause, he added, "But I'd rather have rain than fog. At least we can see."

"Yeah," I agreed. "The rain oughta make stalking real easy. We can walk up and thump 'em on the butt."

Don chuckled as he set his alarm. We had seen only two cows on the trip in, and there were several other machines in the area, more than we'd seen in other years. We hoped the other hunters wouldn't come as far back as our camp. Opening day dawned to drizzling rain. Evidently, the porcupine didn't think much of our campany. It was gone when Tinker checked under the cabin on his way to the outhouse.

Well-breakfasted, we were on the Point, already munching cookies and drinking hot coffee. The moose were scarce, beginning to affirm the Game Board's decision to shorten the season and eliminate nonresident hunters. But by 8:30 we'd seen several cows below us on the golden and pale green flats as well as up high in the bright green alder and dark spruce bands on the hillsides. I went to a spot that allowed me to see the flats as well as most of the hillsides with my binoculars. Tinker and Don chose a spot about fifty yards away that allowed them to see all the hillsides but only about a quarter of the flats.

I heard a scrabble of activity in their direction. I stood to see Don lope toward Tinker with the spotting scope. I waited until the scope was set up and I could tell where they were looking. The low, intense murmur of their voices told me they had seen something promising—perhaps a bull. With my binoculars, I swept the hillside where the scope was aimed, and saw only cows. Then I looked up to the next red ridge beyond where the men appeared to be staring and drew in a shallow breath. A bull! Its rack appeared to be about fifty inches wide. I mentally marked a few reference points, then scooted quietly over to Tinker and Don, following the tree line so I wouldn't look like a walking stick to any animal that might be watching.

"You guys see the bull?" I asked. Their heads spun in unison.

"Bull? We're looking at cows. Where'd you see a bull?" queried Tinker, Don's upturned face mirroring the question. Although it felt good to spot the bull before they did, I didn't gloat. It could just have easily been the other way around.

"He's on the ridge just beyond the cows you're looking at," I said, after kneeling to peer through the scope to be sure of where they were looking.

"See the cows? Now, put them in the bottom of your binoculars at about seven o'clock, and he should be just to the right of middle, right out in the open. His antlers are just out of velvet and real blood-red. He's a little bit to the left of a big clump of tall, green spruce. Look for the clump with no dead trees in it."

"Oh, oh, oh, I see 'im," muttered Tinker. "Let's watch and see what he does. If he lays down, we can just run over there. That's a good spot to get one. Good, good, good."

We waited, keeping an eye on the bull as well as the cows. It was entirely possible that more bulls were lurking in the trees. They don't often stand out in the open, as this fifty-incher was doing. After about fifteen minutes passed and the bull hadn't moved except to casually feed, Tinker decided Don and I should try for him.

"Okay, you saw 'im, go get 'im. Let's see, what's gonna be the best way to get there? You can't go straight in 'cause the cows are in the way, and you won't be able to get past them without spooking 'em. Maybe go down the trail to the creek, then go up it, staying on this bank. It'll take you to the top of the ridge above the cows, and you'll be straight across from him. I'll stay here and flag for you. Whaddya think?" Excitement registered in his voice. The first moose of the season does that to all of us.

"Yeah, except I think it'd be faster to go down the trail to the first low red ridge and go up it, angling in to the creek bank. That's about a half mile closer than the creek. Not as wet, either." I had gone the creek route before, and didn't like it.

"Okay. If you get 'im, start a fire so I can find you in that thick stuff, and I'll come help."

Don and I scurried to divest our day packs of unnecessary stuff like paperback books, bug dope, and the thermos, and checked to be sure we had extra shells, rope, a water jug, and some munch food. A short, hour-long stalk can easily turn into three or four hours, depending on what you encounter en route. I plopped my blue-logoed Alaska Wildlife Safeguard camouflage baseball cap on my head and we were off. The drizzle had stopped, but the bushes held enough water for three rainstorms. Our rain gear earned its keep.

We flew down the hill in our haste to narrow the distance between us and the bull. Unspoken but weighing heavy in the air was the extra pressure of knowing moose were scarce, and the five-day season didn't offer many opportunities or much margin for error. We soon crossed the red ridge, aided by the well-defined game trails zigzagging the area.

Our speedy trek came up short at the rain-flooded creek. The braided, heavily willowed channels that we stepped across last year were no longer visible. A quick glance in both directions told us there was no way across here. Either we had to search up and downstream for a narrower, not so swift crossing, or take our chances that the beaver dam just upstream would be sturdy enough to bear our weight. Not only was it new and very narrow, but it was overflowing as well, thanks to the recent deluges of rain.

We dithered for a moment, then, with a shrug, I balanced my 30.06 in my right hand, glanced back at Don and gingerly stepped off firm ground onto the curved dam. It quaked. Its twenty-yard stretch to the opposite bank looked interminably far away. Slowly, painstakingly, I edged my way along, testing each footstep as I went.

First my left, then my right foot cautiously examined each potential foothold. Some sank under the gentle test, and I wobbled on the spongy, narrow path. No room for error here, and I certainly didn't want to topple, loaded pack, rifle, and all into the bitterly cold water. Nor did I want the water to go over the tops of my leather Cabela's hunting boots. A few more teeters and one last giant step found me on the other bank, completely dry. I turned with a triumphant grin and motioned for Don to come along. He looked doubtful, as uncertain as I had felt taking my first awkward step onto that skinny, undependable walkway. He tottered and wobbled across, not being quite as careful as I because he wore knee-high rubber boots.

Overheated from our hurried walk, we stripped off a shirt layer from under the rain gear. Moving quickly to higher ground, we found a spot where Tinker could see us. We looked through our binoculars for a signal. He had been waiting for us and was ready with our prearranged signal system. The moose was straight to our right. We toiled up the hill, looking and listening as we went, still on the zigzag game trails. Peeking over the top of the knoll, I scanned ahead with my little black Zeiss binoculars. No blood-red-tipped antlers, no bull. No animals at all.

Another signal from Tinker sent us on in the same direction. Twice more of this routine found us on a sparsely treed ridge topped with a foot-wide, hard-packed game trail. We popped up on the ridge behind the only thick patch of Christmas-tree-shaped spruce that could shield us from the next crest. I peered around the edge of the patch toward the opposite ridge, where I was certain the bull should be.

Eureka! Red-tipped antlers barely grazed the tops of the frosted, brilliant red of the dwarf birch. The bull was lying down and didn't know we were looking at him from our hillside. I shrank back behind my spruce shield and excitedly motioned to Don.

We peeked around the tree, shrugging quickly out of our day packs and pink-flagging the tree so we could find it again easily. All trees and ridges here look alike, and more than one backpack has been donated to Mother Nature because its owner neglected to mark its location. We planned to sneak farther along the ridge to a spot that afforded us a more open view of the bull's resting spot. But the moose ruined the plan by heaving to his feet, knowing something in his world was amiss, but not sure what. He stood broadside in the only opening in the trees, head slightly down and looking straight ahead, ears twitching and big, soft nose testing the dampened air currents. A few steps and he would be gone.

Don and I had already slipped shells into the chambers of our rifles. Mine holds four shells, and I always give myself the luxury of a fifth shot by sliding a spare round into the partially opened breech. Snicking the safety off, I whispered over my shoulder to Don, "Back me up," and stepped around the edge of the spruce cover. My rifle already at my shoulder, I squeezed the trigger. I didn't hear the noise and barely felt the recoil.

When I shoot at a moose, the world falls away. But it only happens when I'm hunting, never during target practice. Sometimes I wish it would, to block out distractions.

The bolt and trigger action are so familiar that no thought process is associated with them. Jack a shell out, another in, eyes always on the moose, ready to fire again, the rifle barely leaves my shoulder.

Although I don't think about it, I have three parallel and equally important reasons for my reaction: I don't want to wound the animal, the moose is giving me my dinners for the year to come, and this is a test of my skill. I want to be good. I'm a woman performing in a world that is considered by many to be reserved for males, and I'm not about to blow it.

Watch the moose charge forward, shoot. Jack spent shell out, new one in, hold while the moose spins. Don fires. He sees the moose while I cannot. His second shot, mere seconds later, registers as only a dim roar. I fire a third time, jack the old shell out and a new one in, then wait.

The moose was hidden behind tall yellow willows and scruffy green spruce. We knew from experience he was either dying, his legs thrashing the bushes, or he was crashing through the trees to escape, wounded. Spruce treetops shook and waved vigorously, then all was still. A waiting, penetrating silence descended as we scanned all edges of the brush patch to find any semblance of motion that might signify a wounded animal. There was none.

We each flagged where we'd shot from so we could accurately trace the bullet's trajectory. This usually leads straight to the animal, if your shot has been true. But I worried that the heavy spruce and willow deflected the bullets and that the moose was wounded. Don stayed behind to be my guideline, because the brush was so thick. I forged forward toward the moose's ridge, picking my way across another willow-filled creek. I wandered too far to the left, and Don signaled me back to the right with his hat held aloft at the end of a very straight right arm. I reached the top of the ridge, and Don signaled right again, then lowered his arm and made an odd circular motion. I was puzzled, but he was too far away to ask what it meant, so I had to wait for an answer.

I walked in a grid pattern, listening with tension-sharpened ears, watching for explosive motion at eye level or a motionless dark brown bulk on the ground. Or bright red blood sprayed on the bushes.

Aha! Dark brown bulk on the ground. Motionless, too, I thought to myself. But I was cautious. I've been charged by a "dead" moose before. I circled, watching for the smallest flicker of movement or heaving rib cage. Its open eye was beginning to turn glassy, a sure sign of death, but the true test is to touch the eyeball. If it doesn't react, you know the animal is dead. This is a ticklish task, given that the antlers are generally between you and the eyeball. Each palm on the antler has several tines that can easily poke a neat pattern of holes in your body with a single reflex jerk of the animal's head.

First, I hauled off and kicked the moose in the rear, hard, from the back side. No response. So I circled around to the front, stretching to touch the eyeball with the tip of my rifle barrel. Again no response. Thank goodness.

Quiet no longer, and pleased the moose wasn't wandering around wounded, I trotted around the patch of brush and waved to Don, whose bright red long johns shirt showed up very clearly. He collected our packs and set out toward me at a fast pace.

"Happy birthday to me," I sang to myself as I tied neon-pink flagging on nearby bushes and spruce trees just as high up as I could reach, pulling the more flexible of the trees over to get the survey ribbon to their tops. Just about all of my birthdays have involved hunting, and I delighted in doing the familiar, being outdoors in the crisp fall ambience.

Finishing the flagging that would guide the Bombardier when we came to retrieve the pieced-up moose in a day or so, I returned to the moose, admiring the dinners lying on the ground before me.

But the admiration was bittersweet. The magnificent bull moose wouldn't ever roam these hillsides again, and I did it to him. Life always ends in death, but most people don't confront it head-on, especially as the direct result of their own action, something they are solely and directly responsible for. Hunters deal with it every season, and those of us who guide get it with every hunter.

I sat down on the moose's rump. The still-warm body was full of life only moments ago, and he was king of his world. The cows we saw on the hill below him were probably part of the harem he was collecting for when the mating urge would strike in a week or two. I felt as though I'd cheated him out of years of a fruitful, productive life. I patted the moose on the rear as a way of saying thank you to him. We needed the winter's food, and I'm glad his was a mercifully quick death.

I turned and looked at the Point for Tinker, but he was nowhere to be seen, so I worked on starting a fire. Don appeared, slightly out of breath and grinning.

"How big?" he wanted to know.

"Oh, at least forty-eight inches. I haven't measured." I stopped midstep, suddenly remembering Don's odd circular signal.

"By the way, what was that signal you gave me, when you made those circles with your arm?" I demonstrated, mimicking what I thought his action looked like.

"Dead bird, dead bird. I was telling you that you were right in front of the clump of brush where I thought the moose went down, and all I could think of was 'dead bird, dead bird.' You know how a dead bird falls, spiraling on its way down."

"Oh." I had to think about that for a moment, and then the idea of a huge moose acting like a dead bird struck me as pretty funny. I giggled.

"How far a shot do you think that was?" Don wondered.

"My guess is about 200 yards." I glanced around, then looked toward where we had dropped our packs, noting how thick the willows and spruce were. I bet myself that some of our shots were deflected by the brush.

Tinker came huffing up, grinning as widely as Don and I.

"Good job! He settled down about five minutes after you left, so I just waited for you two to show up. I could see exactly where you shot, and where he ran to. I waited until you found him before I took off to come over here. Let's get to work!"

"Is your tape measure handy?" I asked. "Mine is buried in my pack, and I want to know how big he is."

"Yeah," Tinker said. "Got it right here. Okay, this looks like the farthest out point, stretch across to here. Hold that end, would you? Okay, it looks like—by golly, I guessed right on! Fifty-one inches."

Two hours later the moose was skinned, quartered, and hung in a nearby tree. While we were tying a log horizontally between two spruce to form a sturdy hanging pole, Tinker began to cackle.

"You guys shot a Boone and Crockett spruce! Look at this. I saw this freshly broken branch, and I knew I hadn't cut it. Then up here I found the bullet hole in the tree trunk."

As we skinned the moose, we discovered that only one of our five shots even hit the moose, and it turned out to be my first shot, when he'd been facing uphill. All the rest had been fired when he was moving downhill. Shows what a moving target and brush deflection can do to usually good shots. Fortunately,

Don Wanie with a nice moose, 1989.

the first one was well-placed, going through the top of a lung, breaking a rib and, most importantly, breaking the bull's spine. None of the other shots were necessary, but only the skinning and cleaning process revealed that. Knowing it had been a difficult shot, I was pleased.

On the third day of the season, Tinker's and Don's shared moose was hanging in camp with mine. On the fourth day, we closed up Point Camp and headed for Green Cabin to check on Bob and Peggy's success.

We wondered why Wayne and the crew in the other Bombardier had never appeared, so we looked for them as we trundled along, but to no avail. When we parted company several days earlier, we had agreed on a time the first evening to try to talk to each other on our CB radios. We called Wayne, but got no audible response. We thought they heard us, though, because we could hear the noise of their transmitter when they keyed the microphone to speak. Wayne told us later that we came though crystal-clear, but their transmitter had indeed malfunctioned.

Late afternoon brought a steady downpour. We found Bob and Peggy in the cabin drying off, steaming cups of coffee in hand. They quickly supplied us with our own hot cups of coffee, and added a shot of brandy to warm us completely through. They had the ratio of coffee to brandy down pat. But they hadn't found a legal moose yet. And they'd not seen the other half of our crew either. They said the tracked vehicle traffic was almost continuous, though, and we were certain it had contributed to their lack of success. No animals will stay around a noisy, heavily populated place.

We hung our two moose so their glazing process would continue, making sure the tarps were positioned to keep rain from falling on the dark red pieces. All five of us piled in the cabin for a garlic and onion and moose tenderloin dinner, accompanied by garden-fresh potatoes and carrots and followed by the last of the brandy. The brandy warmed the very pit of our stomachs and spread the glow all the way to our toes.

The last day of the season promised to be all-time awful. Morning arrived without a let-up in the rain. On top of the hill behind the cabin we huddled inside our hoods, alternately drying binocular lenses and scanning the countryside. Only cows, and very few at that, so we decided to walk to a hill about two miles away that would give us a much wider view. After building peanut butter and jelly sandwiches and warming up with coffee, we set out through the rainsoaked woods for the far hill. But between us and our destination was a very swift, swollen creek that had to be crossed twice to get there, then crossed twice more to get back.

Downed trees that had fallen across the creek gave us our crossings, but they weren't very safe. Nobody wanted to take the first step. Finally, Bob decided he'd go, since he had crossed on the logs several times before the water got so swift and deep. Each tree was about thirty feet long and probably three feet around at the butt. We inched our way across the rain-slickened wood and bark, using branches for support and ignoring the rushing water tugging at the submerged branches, making the tree bounce erratically in the roiling water. Where there were no branches on top, we balanced ourselves with arms out, rifles held tightly. One slip and drowning was possible. Our packs catching on sweepers hidden under the water would help assure that. I remembered a friend telling me about falling in a fast, wide creek when he was sheep hunting. He was under water until he thought his lungs would burst before he was finally able to struggle out of his pack. This water was violently fast and looked treacherous. Where it had been only a foot deep, it now roared five and six feet deep, and new channels formed in the gullies. Hidden in all that water were willow and alder bushes to snare people and backpacks.

Spending the entire afternoon on the hill didn't offer any better results than the morning, except that we could see the trail and were able to count four all-terrain vehicles leaving the area. Hunting season was winding down.

So we made two more creek crossings, hearts thudding. It took sheer will-power to set foot back onto those slippery tree trunks, but it was the only way home to the cabin and to warmth. The rain, which hadn't let up, chilled us to the core.

The next morning we hit the trail. The normal creek crossing was too deep and treacherous for the Bombardier, so we searched out a shallower crossing. For miles, water ran ahead of us in the trail where, at least in our memory, no water had run before. It was the worst Tinker and I had ever seen.

The others didn't know enough about the country to be aware of the consequences, but I was not looking forward to crossing the Middle Fork of the Gulkana River. I knew Tinker was also worried, because he was being the quintessential back seat driver. Nothing I could do was right. I wanted to snap back at him, but I knew why he was being crabby so I held my tongue.

At a rest stop, I finally voiced my worries, and the conversation made the party fall silent.

"Tinker, what do you think the Middle Fork crossing's gonna be like?" I watched for his reaction.

"I don't like the looks of this. If it's too deep or running too fast, we might have to camp 'till it goes down. I don't want to lose us or the equipment. We just might all be a day or two late getting back to work." Tension clipped off his words and made his actions a little jerky.

The group's eyes went round. Water running in the trail faster than the Bombardier moved along was enough to give us pause, and the thought of a very full

Middle Fork silenced us. We also knew we had to make the rest of the five-hour trip out beyond the Middle Fork without being sucked into a mudhole. Remembering how dry the previous fall had been, I shook my head.

When we reached the top of the bluff that plunged the trail down to the valley flats through which the Middle Fork coursed, we stopped to look. The trails below were shimmering, gray-glinting ribbons woven through the defoliated willows and the rain-darkened spruce. They appeared to be all water. We soon found they were indeed very full of water, running a foot deep.

The Middle Fork roared twenty feet wider in some places. The channels had changed, and deep holes formed where none had been only seven days before. We piled out of the Bombardier and hurried to inspect the rushing river. A Nodwell and three four-wheelers were on the opposite bank, and two men were winching across a fourth four-wheeler. In a short conversation with the man on our bank of the river, we discovered that the Nodwell had washed 150 yards downstream on their first crossing attempt. We never did discover how or where they crossed, except that they had to use their winch. We also knew that the second channel of the river crossing was deep but passable. They had already crossed it twice, ferrying four-wheelers.

We spent two hours searching for a secure crossing.

"Tinker, do you want to borrow my hip boots?" I wanted to walk out to see how far a couple of the gravel bars went, but Tinker wouldn't hear of it. He took me up on my boot-borrowing offer, though, and ended up wearing them for nearly two hours. My feet are three sizes smaller than his, so when he kept them on for so long I knew he was concerned about our crossing predicament. Finally, he found a spot that was safe as far out as he could walk. But we couldn't tell how deep the water was at the opposite bank. So, opting for even greater safety, we yelled and waved to get the attention of the men with the machine on the opposite bank. When they finally figured out we wanted to talk to them, they drove toward the riverbank.

We hollered, asking if they could hook up their winch to power us across the river in case we fell in a hole or were swept downstream. We threw a rope over, which they tied to the winch cable's hook. Tinker hauled it back to us and connected it to the front of the Bombardier. Don and I tied a tarp to the heavy mesh radiator cover above the winch hook. The goal was to keep the engine from being drowned into stalling by the water we were about to plunge into. We put plywood sideboards in the open doors of the cab to keep a deluge of water from pouring through. Tinker drove, and the remaining four of us huddled in the back, wide-eyed and adrenaline coursing.

"Stay below the cab. If that cable snaps, it'll take your head off." Don's construction experience was showing. We all ducked down, but remained facing forward. We were going to face our demise, if it was really going to happen.

The Bombardier in granny gear, Tinker floored the gas pedal. The machine shuddered on the gravel bar, gained and lost traction, but forged ahead through the six-foot-deep water. We aimed for a spot thirty yards upstream from our intended destination on the opposite bank, and ended up ten yards downstream from it. The force of the water was strong enough to push four tons of machine loaded with at least another two tons of people, moose, trailer, tools, and gear forty yards downstream. No holes swallowed us up, and we actually drove across under our own power. But there's no denying the psychological advantage the winch gave us. Without it, we wouldn't have attempted to cross the raging water. We would have climbed back up the steep hill to get away from the ponds and creek-filled trails on the valley floor to camp until the water subsided enough for us to cross.

When we reached the opposite bank, big grins of relief appeared on everyone's face. We hopped out and shook hands, babbling thank-you's to our helpers. They were happy to lend a hand. Someone else had helped them earlier, and they wanted to pass the favor along.

Tinker was positively giddy. Still in my too-small hip boots, he went around to the front of his Bombardier and kissed it. Not once, but twice. And then once again for good measure.

"What a wonderful machine! Didn't she do great? We never even broke away from the bottom." He was beside himself. Finally he realized his feet hurt, and got out of my boots. Then it was my turn to be on the receiving end of a kiss. Don, who was standing next to me, ran. He didn't want to be included in Tinker's kiss fest.

Wayne, Don, Babe, and Sam still hadn't appeared by the time we were ready to leave for home the next morning. I found out later their trip was full of problems. Rain kept them inside their tent for most of two days, and they broke a track tightener, limiting their ability to drive. These Bombardiers steer with a braking action; that is, pulling the left steering lever inside the cab stops the left track, causing the machine to turn in that direction. Similarly, pulling the right steering lever makes it turn right. First they whittled a piece of wood to wedge between the rear axle and the track tightener base on the body of the machine, but the first few revolutions of the track crushed it. So they limped along to their first campsite and set up living quarters. The next day they hunted, ignoring their lack of mobility. Getting a moose that day, though, forced them to fix the problem. It's not a good idea to leave fresh meat unattended for very long, because bears firmly believe in the adage that possession is nine-tenths of the law.

Wayne pondered the situation and, in his true genius fashion, built a forge. While Babe tended the roaring fire, Wayne and Don took turns hacksawing the appropriate length of solid metal from the winch base. They alternately heated and pounded the ends of the thick metal bar into a rounded depression that eventually fit around the axle. It took six hours of effort, and it wasn't a perfect fit, but they were able to finish hunting and drive all the way out.

Not having hunters turned out to be a pleasure. We didn't have to get up before dawn every single day. We all stayed in the cabin with the wood stove, sleeping in bunks instead of being in the tent on the ground, sleeping on Thermarest pads. And we cooked dinner whenever we wanted. We were irreverent, rude, and silly without worrying about offending anyone. We also took time out to chain saw a hole in the log wall and put a window in the cabin, letting light in without having to keep the door open. Rainy days indoors became immensely more pleasant. For me, the only drawback to the whole trip was having to choose between going with Wayne, Don, Babe, and Sam, or with Tinker, Don, Peggy, and Bob.

Babe Evans with a good meat moose, 1986.

Trouble In Paradise

As MICHAEL, ALONG AS packer and helper, and I waited in the unseasonably hot sun at Island Lake for the first set of the season's moose hunters, I chattered about the coming hunt. I was looking forward to this season. After years of assistant-guiding and running my own camp, this was the first year with my registered guide's license. Besides having Michael as a helper, I was to have Carol Sisk as cook. Although he could only stay for the first half of this hunt, I also had Lynn Levengood as an assistant guide. Mike Tinker and Wayne Hanson hired them because there was no way I could guide three individual hunters, keep the camp organized, haul water, cook, do dishes, maintain the Bombardier, and do a good job of everything.

Carol was the only person we'd ever had whose sole responsibility was cooking, besides Melissa and me. Although she hadn't cooked for a hunting camp before, she and her husband Steve, both near fifty, hunt and camp regularly, so she was familiar with outdoor living. I met Carol through Steve; he and I work for the same state agency when I'm not guiding. I welcomed her company. Blonde and softspoken, she created tasty dishes from our abundant variety of canned and dried food. Although we had plenty of canned meats, vegetables, and fruit, as well as rice and macaroni, potatoes, bread, peanut butter and jelly, and munchy day pack food, the amount of fresh meat was limited. Typically, a successful hunter provides fresh meat within the first three days of a hunt, but that was not to be with the three hunters we were waiting for.

Lynn, a friend of Pete Buist's and an attorney full-time, holds an assistant guide license as a sideline. Brown-haired and about five feet eight inches tall, he turned out to be a quiet and capable woodsman with a dry sense of humor.

The three hunters were from Detroit, and I knew two of them. Stan, a stocky silver-haired restaurant owner in his early fifties, had hunted with me and other guides the year before at this camp as one of a party of four, which had included Hank.

Hank didn't come this year because of a family illness, but sent his twenty-one-year-old son (whom we came to call "The Kid"). Hank paid for the trip because he wanted his son to experience the outdoors and to see something besides the inside of bars. Doing some quick mental addition, I surmised that Hank must have invested around eight thousand dollars in his son's hunt, figuring the cost of the hunt itself, non-resident license and tags, airfare, hotel bills, and gear.

The third person this year was Tom, a business associate of Hank's. Each year, Hank arranged a hunting trip for one or two of his business associates. Tom was the buyer Hank worked with at a company that supplied his steel tank fabrication company with materials. I didn't know anything else about Tom, except he was a big man. I'd soon find out how big.

"Michael," I said, "if these guys are anything like last year's bunch, we ought to have a fun time. We've already seen moose, so if we can get these guys close enough to shoot, we ought to have full tickets before a week is over."

"I thought you said Hank drank a lot last year," he replied. "Was he an okay hunter?"

"Oh, yes," I replied. "He was a good hunter. Knew about being quiet. Knew what to wear in the brush, and he was so good-natured. You could tell he was the leader of the crew. He did drink too much, but he was a happy drunk. He became an alcoholic because he thought he had to take his clients and buyers out wining, dining, and partying. Then it got the better of him and he couldn't stop."

I sat, momentarily somber, thinking about Hank. Last year, he had to have a drink at regular intervals or he would get the shakes so badly he couldn't function. When he and I were alone on a hillside, we talked about drinking and alcoholism and drink-related health problems. I told him some about my father's alcoholism and death, and he told me about his fears of dying too soon to see his kids and grandkids grow up. He confided at the end of his hunt that he was going home to dry out.

"And you know what," I went on, "Hank went home and got dried out. When I went to Detroit this summer, he took Mother, Uncle Ed, and me out to dinner and he was sober as could be. He had a Diet Coke. He said he was gonna be sober the rest of his life.

"But I think his son drinks a fair amount. When I met him this summer, it was around noon and he still had the shakes from being out partying. I hope he figures out why Hank quit before he gets to that point."

I paused, then went on. "The Kid kept saying he wouldn't like it up here. He wanted to stay in Detroit because he didn't think he could stand being away from the city. He likes noise and action. I think he'll enjoy it once he gets here, though. The country's too beautiful not to win him over."

As we later found out, the young man didn't care a whit for the outdoors. He was twenty-one, dark-haired, bright-eyed, good looking, and wanted to be back in Detroit going to nightclubs and chasing girls.

"What's Stan like?" Michael wanted to know. "Is he in good shape? Can he walk well enough to handle the brush and the hills?"

"He did fine last year," I replied. "He doesn't hear real well, though, and his clothes were noisy. He wore Carhartts, and you know how loud the brush is scraping on that canvas duck material.

"What I do worry about," I continued, "is last year Stan shot his moose once, then just stood and stared when it didn't fall over. I told him a couple times to shoot again and either he didn't hear me, or he didn't think he needed to shoot. I ended up having to shoot when the moose started to run, 'cause the guy was standing there with his mouth open. I hope he remembers to keep shooting this year." I grinned. "Got that sucker right under the ear on a dead run. He dropped like he'd been pole-axed."

Stan had been upset that I'd shot his moose, so I explained Alaska's wanton waste laws to him again, letting him know that it was my responsibility not to let a moose get away if a hunter had already wounded it. I think he understood. I also think his sense of macho was wounded.

Soon Wayne had everybody and their gear delivered to Island Lake. Tom, the last to arrive, filled the co-pilot's seat next to Wayne, dwarfing him. A Special Forces Marine in Vietnam, Tom came away from the war with many decorations from jungle reconnaissance missions. Trained to kill, he was not a man to argue with. His palms were easily six inches across, he was about six feet five inches tall, and looked like he weighed 350 pounds. Dark haired and swarthy, he was good-hearted and cheerful, but gave the underlying impression he could be menacing.

We loaded the Bombardier and headed for camp. Michael and I had already set up a tent for the crew, opened the cabin, and organized the cooking area for Carol. In the crew tent, our army cots were so rickety from use that we wedged three of them against each other in a U-shape, one along each wall and at the back of the tent. The fourth person would sleep on pads on the ground in the center. We tied the cot legs together to stabilize the wiggles, which later prompted Carol to joke that if a bear got one of us, all three would go bouncing through the bushes like link sausages.

At Point Camp, I went over gun safety, discussed the need for quiet, waiting for the guide's signal to shoot, wanton waste, and sundry other hunt and camp rules. Stan knew the daily drill of getting up, downing breakfast, packing lunches, and walking to the Point, so he tried to help keep The Kid and Tom on track. His hearing was worse than the year before, though, and he didn't know how loud his voice could get when he talked. We had to keep reminding all three hunters to keep their voices down. And none of the men were in good enough physical shape to walk much. The terrain was steep and the brush was thick, but separating the men and walking was likely going to be the only way to find a moose in the hot weather if they insisted on being so noisy while they sat and looked.

Besides being in poor physical condition, the men wore noisy clothing, which hindered hiking and stalking. While The Kid and Tom could strip out of their harsh-sounding outer gear when they got close enough for a stalk, Stan's clothing was a problem. He hadn't remembered anything about quiet clothes. He wore new canvas duck pants with nylon on the fronts of the legs, which he couldn't strip out of, and a canvas duck jacket. Branches scraping on new canvas duck sound like a stick scratching a wooden wall, and on nylon, they make an indescribable swooshing noise. Fabrics like wool, polar fleece, even blue jeans are quieter than canvas. They let the hunter duplicate the sound of branches on animal hair. I began to have doubts about an immediately successful hunt.

On the second night, the weather was still and clear. Still enough that we could hear the loons on Island Lake hooting plaintively, and so clear that the northern lights looked as though they would land on our heads if they dropped any lower in the sky. I knocked on the cabin door to let the hunters know the aurora was out. The only one to get up was The Kid, who was so enthralled he tried to take pictures with his point-and-shoot camera. He and I shivered together while I tried to explain the aurora phenomenon.

On about the third day, we spotted an empty half-gallon Jack Daniels bottle in the garbage. Although I did wonder, at times, why The Kid fell heavily asleep as soon as we reached a spotting place and stayed asleep for two or three hours, it didn't occur to us that only one person was drinking. We thought all three clients were participating.

About a third of the way into the hunt, I opted to take Tom, The Kid, and Lynn across the valley in the Bombardier. We hoped to spot a big bull moose we had seen there the evening before. It was in nearly the same spot, so Tom and I began a stalk.

"Tom, stay behind me, but be ready. The brush is so thick here, you may not have much of a chance to shoot." I didn't think to remind him he should wait until I signaled to shoot.

The moose had risen from its bed and was standing on the crest of the slope we were on. He wasn't sure what had disturbed him, and was standing still, ears twitching and turning, trying to locate us. I began to motion Tom into the brush so we could sneak closer when a shot exploded just behind me. The moose hunched up, then erupted and disappeared down the hill.

Like Stan the year before, Tom was accustomed to shooting deer, which fall over at a shot from a large caliber rifle. Not so with moose, especially if you hit an antler. An antler shot can knock a moose down and stun him, or send him off like this one. We looked for a bit, but saw no blood and gave up. By the time we quit looking, Lynn and The Kid appeared.

"We missed," I told them. "I think Tom managed to get the antler."

"Yeah," said Tom. "I had no idea they could move so fast. I never even had time for a second shot." He sounded disappointed.

"You'll have other chances," I said. "Just chalk this up to a learning experience." And I quietly explained again why the hunters should wait for the guide's signal to shoot. I had hoped to voice-call the moose to settle him down, then move us closer for a more certain shot.

As we headed back to the Bombardier, we heard shooting. Michael, Stan, and Carol were on the Point, in the direction the shooting came from, but the shots sounded much farther away, so we didn't pay attention.

When we returned after a couple hours, we learned that after Tom shot, our moose ran like a freight train away from us and around the front of the Point. The crew on the point saw it and Stan emptied his rifle and then Michael's rifle into it. The moose, full of adrenalin, didn't fall. Instead, it charged off into the brush, zigzagging down the hill and away.

"Carol saw it over there," Michael said as he pointed toward a finger of timber, "but I could swear it went over there," swinging his arm to the left. "We've gone down and looked, but the brush is real thick. We need help."

"Did you hang some flagging so we know where Stan shot from? And how about the places where you think you each last saw the moose?"

Searching for the big bull was going to be a chore. The area was full of hummocks, dips, thick brush, and patches of heavy timber. Wounded moose can run for miles.

They had flagged, so we began working a grid pattern, all seven of us spread about twenty yards apart, keeping voice contact. We searched about a mile down the hill in nearly a three-quarter-mile-wide swath for six more hours, to no avail. It was almost too dark to see, so I called the search off.

"If Wayne flies over tomorrow, we'll ask him to fly a grid to see if he can spot it from the air. In the meantime, let's keep an eye out for camp robbers and ravens zeroing in on a spot down here. They should show us where the moose is."

Stan sighed heavily. This moose was much bigger than the one he'd shot last year. He wanted the meat, I knew, and he wanted the larger rack even more.

"Stan," I said, "all we can do at this point is wait to see if Wayne finds your moose tomorrow."

"I really want that moose," Stan said. He looked distracted.

The next day, Wayne wasn't able to see the moose either. Good fortune wasn't with us.

As time went on, we soon realized that Tom was the only one who had much hunting experience, probably as a result of Marine Special Forces training, where stealth meant your life. Even though Stan had been here the year before, he apparently hadn't retained much. Tom remembered to stay quiet until the conversation of the other two would get the better of him and he would be drawn in. Constant reminding didn't do much good. It dawned on me that Stan followed the lead of his friends. Last year, Hank kept a firm rein on everyone, including their hunting etiquette, but this year, his influence was missing. For some reason, The Kid seemed to dominate, perhaps because Stan and Tom were friends of Hank's.

Although entranced by the northern lights and the enormous vastness of the woods, The Kid couldn't stand being quiet. He got angry at his little radio-cassette player because it wouldn't pick up any radio stations and he'd forgotten to bring tapes. He was angry because his father hadn't told him radio stations couldn't reach where we were. He threw the player in the garbage; I retrieved it, and now it plays FM radio stations and tapes in my office.

The Kid was also angry because we hadn't brought enough fresh meat to last the full ten days. It didn't occur to him that it would spoil because we didn't have any way to refrigerate it.

He began to stay at the cabin in the mornings while Carol cleared away the breakfast remains, and several times he returned to the cabin in the middle of the day. If Stan went with him, loud conversations would waft down the hill. If he went back by himself, we would still hear him talking. The moose we had seen moved farther and farther away until they disappeared altogether. Tom and Stan had each had good chances for moose at the beginning of the ten days, and both lost out for different reasons.

The Kid had no opportunities to shoot at all, and I think it ate at him. Soon a second empty half-gallon of Jack Daniels appeared, followed by an empty quart of vodka and an empty fifth of whiskey. We discovered that Stan and Tom had only a drink or two in the evening. That meant The Kid was downing the rest. Our eyebrows went up. Alcohol and guns don't mix, no matter how well trained a person is about firearms. I know from first-hand experience. Daddy had some bouts with the bottle and twice put holes in our log house. Even though he received top marksmanship and rifle safety awards in the Army, alcohol made him careless. Knowing that The Kid had little experience with guns scared me spitless. From then on, we made sure the rifles were empty as soon as we got back to camp.

Each day, we constantly reminded the men to be quiet. Tom tried to help, but he often got caught up in the others' activity.

In the crew tent, the situation was a nightly topic. It was obvious we weren't going to find any moose near the Point. None of us knew how to convince the hunters to be quieter, and we had all arrived at the conclusion that The Kid was the root of the problem. He talked most to Carol, mother of two teenagers, when he stayed at the cabin while she cleaned up after breakfast. She thought he was confused about life.

We realized The Kid was intelligent. Although he had no education beyond high school, he was responsible for computer applications in his father's business. One of the software developers used his input to create a program the steel tank fabrication business needed. It bothered me that the young man chose to drown his capabilities in alcohol. But right then I was more frustrated by his attitude about being quiet and by his immediate effect on the other two hunters.

"Well, I wouldn't let The Kid smoke in my pickup on the way down here," Lynn said. "Maybe that got him off on the wrong foot." He paused, then added, "Do they realize you guys have more hunters coming in, and all their noise is driving the game away? The next group might not have anything to even look at."

I'd thought about that, and had decided we'd go farther back in and set up a tent camp if we had to. Moose could be found. A few days' worth of quiet, and they might even reappear again here.

We all tried to figure out how to get the men to be quiet. Each morning, I'd try a new tactic. One day, gentleness. The next day, a blunt, direct reminder. Then, on the next-to-last day, we awoke to The Kid yelling. He wasn't conversing, he was yelling. Lynn had flown out on schedule, leaving me with all three men to guide. Carol and Michael helped as much as they could, but I let the responsibility weigh heavily on me. My frustration about the unsatisfactory hunt bubbled into a seething boil. I yanked open my sleeping bag, jumped into my clothes, and burst into the cabin. I was so angry that I was shaking.

"You guys," I yelled. "You've ruined your chances of shooting a moose by being so noisy. I've tried and tried and tried to ask you, to tell you, to be quiet, and you don't seem to care. Well, besides screwing up your own hunt, I hope you know you may have ruined the hunt here for the next group that's coming in."

I whirled to head out the door, then turned back around, jabbing my index finger at them.

"If any of you want to go, I'll take the Bombardier to try a new area. This is your last day, so make up your minds if you want to come with me or not." I stomped out, leaving a silent cabin behind me.

Stan and The Kid opted not to go. They were afraid we wouldn't get back in time to go to Island Lake the next day so they could leave when Wayne flew in to get them. They thought that if the Bombardier broke down away from camp, they might have to walk all the way to the road, and worried because they didn't know which way to go. They worried that Wayne might forget to arrive at the lake to pick them up. I tried to allay their fears, explaining that the only thing that could prevent Wayne from coming was the weather. I pointed out the hill I planned to try that day, and explained that if the Bombardier broke down away from camp, we could still backpack their gear to Island Lake. But they were angry and worried, so they stayed behind with Carol.

Tom, Michael, and I went. Tom relaxed as soon as we were out of sight of camp. It took about an hour of driving to reach the high hill. We spent a peaceful, albeit somewhat tense, day. Being away from the noisemakers was wonderful. The strain of wanting to find a moose for Tom, though, kept nagging at me.

I left Michael and Tom to look at the easterly valley, and went to look the opposite direction. Finally I stopped in a clearing about a mile away from the two men and sat down, leaning against a small tree. For a while I just slumped and stared at the countryside below me. It felt good. I needed to be away from everybody.

Eventually, I picked up my binoculars and began to look. Over the course of an hour, several cow moose meandered through the green alders in the distance. I kept watching for a bull to appear. According to the laws of nature and the pending rut, at least one bull should certainly be around all those cows.

With no warning, a piercing scream ripped the air and then stopped. I involuntarily jerked the binoculars away from my eyes. Where had the noise come from? It seemed to be just yards below my clearing. It started again, too big for a rabbit but about right for one of this year's moose calves. The scream went on and on and on, seeming not to stop for a breath, then stopped as abruptly as it began, cut off in mid-scream. I managed to pinpoint the hillside about a mile away as the location of the blood-curdling sound.

I shivered, feeling suddenly cold in the hot autumn sun. An animal had just died. Had a wolf or a bear killed something? What mystery did those willows and spruce hide? I'd never find the spot if I looked for a million years, so my curiosity had to go unanswered.

Moments after, I heard rushing four-legged footsteps behind me, coming toward me. "Bear!" rushed through my mind. I grabbed my rifle and jumped up, confronting a lone large, white-maned bull caribou. As astonished as I was, it leaped straight up in the air, galloped over the crest of the hill, and disappeared from sight. Still shaken and chilled from listening to the scream, I was completely rattled by the noisy caribou. It was time to rejoin Michael and Tom.

Although we saw one bull moose at close range, it was spooky and ran before Tom was able to find it in his scope, so we returned to a quieter camp empty-handed. That night, no one was in a particularly jovial mood, so we all retired early. After breakfast the next day, we loaded the Bombardier and headed for Island Lake. The Kid headed for the airplane without a backward glance. Carol, Tom, and then Michael went on the next flights, while Stan waited for the last trip.

"Sharon," Stan began when we were finally by ourselves, "I was insulted when you yelled at us yesterday morning. You didn't have to yell at me."

A curious caribou in the Alphabet Hills.

"Stan, I apologize. But I hope you understand that being noisy ruined your chances of getting a moose." I was sorry I'd lost my temper, but I still wanted him to understand why being quiet was necessary. We talked until Wayne reappeared, clearing the air and parting friends.

What a mess this hunt had turned into. I'd been wondering for days why I ever bothered to get a guide's license.

"Have a rough hunt?" Wayne asked, once Stan was in the plane. The glint in his eye said he understood. "Was that kid trouble?"

"Oh, he was kind of a pain." I rolled my eyes, shaking my head. "They were pretty noisy." Understatement has always been my forte.

He climbed in the plane and flew off. I stood on the shore, watching the last of my misery disappear, hoping Wayne was right that the next four hunters would be more fun. He'd better be, or I was really going to regret becoming a guide.

The season was over and I was back in my office when Melissa, my friend and ex-assistant guide, bustled in and plopped in my visitor's chair. She and her boyfriend, Jim Owen, had been at Tangle Lakes when Wayne flew our hunters in from the field. They got to see the fireworks first-hand.

"Okay, what's the story with that young obnoxious hunter?" she asked. "Did you know Naidine threw him out of the lodge?"

Naidine and her husband Jack run Tangle River Inn, a lodge and bar across from Tinker and Wayne's Tangle Lakes base camp. Naidine knows no strangers; she is gregarious, funny, notices everything, and has an imposing presence, kin to a pint-sized version of Refrigerator Perry. The Kid had to have behaved pretty badly to get the heave-ho from her.

"Well, as I got the story from Naidine," Melissa explained, "he was in there ranting and raving about what a lousy hunting operation you guys run, how it was awful out in camp, and nobody ever found him anything to shoot at. Then he started in on what idiots Wayne and Tinker are, and I think that was the straw that broke the camel's back. Naidine doesn't like sourpusses, but she'll take their money. What she couldn't stand was that kid bad-mouthing you and Tinker and Wayne. So she told him to leave, and you know you don't argue with Naidine!"

Melissa and I laughed.

"Well, I'm impressed." I thought for a moment. "Did The Kid say much about being in the field?"

"He disappeared straight over to the lodge and started hitting the sauce. After Naidine kicked him out, he got pretty scary. Jim was about ready to throw him in the lake." Melissa grimaced at the memory.

"The Kid yelled right in Tom's face, calling him all sorts of names. He had a fit because he thought Tom got better treatment and kept screaming at him it was his fault the hunt was awful. I'm surprised Tom didn't punch his lights out. All he did, though, was stare straight out over The Kid's head. After that, The Kid staggered off to one of the cabins and passed out. What a sad case."

Melissa paused, then ended with, "Boy, what a helluva way to initiate your guide's license."

Hindsight offers such humbling clarity. I should have realized The Kid couldn't stand silence—he'd even told me so, indirectly, during my summer visit to Detroit—and he certainly acted it out during the hunt.

I also should have figured out that he probably had a physical addiction to alcohol. After he ran out of things to drink, his nerves began to fray and his emotions tilted out of balance. I should have gone for a walk with him, away from the others, to see if he'd talk about how he was feeling and behaving. Instead, I let myself get agitated and upset. Next time, I'd know better.

Walking Softly

"One does not hunt in order to kill—one kills in order to have hunted."

Jose Ortega y Gasset, *Meditations on Hunting*

NOT ALL HUNTS TURN OUT happily. Some hunters have pursued only small game before and don't understand that larger caliber rifles are necessary for big game. Some think they already know it all because they've hunted other deer-family animals in the Lower 48. Some don't want to be led by a woman guide but haven't admitted it to themselves yet. Others don't know about being quiet—and don't choose to learn. Try as I might, the concept of silence, blending in, and paying attention to the animals—in short, hunting—doesn't get through. I sit on the hillside, powerless and frustrated, binoculars to my eyes, watching as each day the animals drift farther and farther away, until several days into the hunt they've moved around the mountain and are seven to ten miles away, far out of range.

Some hunters don't want to walk, to stalk the animal they've come so far for; they want it to be close, to come to them. These hunters leave dissatisfied because they didn't bag "their" trophy. They will lay blame everywhere except on their own lack of skills. It's often convenient for them to imply that the reason they didn't bag an animal is that "that girl" was their guide.

These are also the hunters who haven't realized that a hunt is what they make it; they haven't discovered that the big trophy and the killing are but a small part of the art of hunting. It's small consolation to know that my guide partners (actually, nearly all guides) experience the same thing from time to time. Particularly frustrating is knowing how easy it is to have a good hunt and to enjoy Alaska. I dearly want for people to leave a hunt in Alaska satisfied, pleased with their experience, charmed by the solitude and the nearness of wild animals, and with a sense of wonder at the beauty of the wilderness.

In the recent past, I worked with Pete Buist, guiding some hunters from New Mexico in the Brooks Range. Two men, Wendel and Mark, had come for Dall sheep and grizzly bear, and Mark bought black bear and moose tags as well.

Their friend Sam came along—not to hunt, but for the experience. Pete hired Bill, a young Texan he'd met during a Fairbanks Boy Scout trip to Texas, to be our packer. Bill had just finished college and was realizing one of his dreams by coming to Alaska. He arrived with a big grin on his lean face and a sense of humor to back it up. Good thing. Near the hunt's end, Pete good-naturedly embarrassed Bill by presenting him, in a tent-front ceremony, with a fur-lined jock strap and naming him Son of Bone, aka SOB, award. Pete elaborated on Bill's hard work, ability to smile through our teasing, and to mercilessly let us have it with dry rejoinders.

Saying that Wendel got a grizzly and Mark came away with a moose and a cinnamon bear (a color phase of the black bear) makes it sound like the hunt went well. In some ways, it did. The weather let the Super Cub deliver all of us in one day to a small gravel bar in the creek adjacent to camp, and the next day dawned clear and sunny. Hiking up a mountain creek to find sheep, Bill and Wendel slipped on the rocks and fell in a couple times, but dried quickly in the warm air. When we found no sheep by midafternoon, Pete took Mark and Bill on a successful stalk for the cinnamon bear we'd seen early that day. Wendel and I hunted our way back to camp to find Sam and get dinner ready.

Bill Miller discovers that he is about to become the proud owner of a fur-lined jock strap, presented by Pete Buist. August 1992.

Each day, the weather turned colder and windier. My half-full quart water bottle froze every night in my tent, Mark injured his Achilles tendons and had trouble walking in his boots, and the mountain tributaries draining into our bigger creek all turned to ice. On the day that Wendel got his grizzly, Pete did a back flip (complete with Olympic high-dive ratings and commentary from his companions) over an iced mountain creek and landed so hard on the rocks that we thought he'd broken a rib. He was out of commission for the rest of the hunt. Mike, Sam's son, was hunting off the Alaska Highway with a friend of Pete's, Dave Bridges, a pilot who was then an assistant guide. They were supposed to fly in to join us midway through our hunt, but each evening came without them. We learned later that an unseasonably early and heavy snowfall in Fairbanks kept Dave's plane grounded.

The weather turned stormy and dumped snow on us for a day and a half in a howling wind. It forced us to turn a big blue tarp into an arctic entry for the cooktent, which was the communal gathering place—it had a wood stove and a table. Then we had to change the angle of the arctic entry when the wind shifted to keep the snow from boiling in and the tent from billowing with cold air.

The men were disappointed because we weren't able to get to the sheep, especially Mark, who also had his heart set on a grizzly. Sam, who was on his first trip to Alaska and who was not much of an outdoors person, worried more each day

Ice fall in the Brooks Range near the site of Pete Buist's Olympic-rated tumble; 1992. Photo taken by Bill Miller.

Mike and Dave didn't appear. But through it all, although they could have turned sour and grumpy, they laughed and joked and told stories and teased each other and us. I would head for my tent each night with my cheeks' laugh muscles aching. They helped bring in wood and haul water and took turns cooking, giving us a taste of their home-grown chilies and a few recipes that hooked our appetites completely.

"Sometimes chicken, sometimes feathers," is how Mark put it. When you snatch in the henhouse for a chicken, sometimes all you come away with is a handful of feathers. That's how it is hunting. Both Wendel and Mark were experienced enough to know that and not to let it ruin their whole trip. The blizzard didn't dampen their spirits. Bill spent part of the first evening of the storm out in it, breathing deeply, walking to the creek to look up and downstream, and taking pictures of the blowing snow.

These men endured tough hunt conditions with class. They enjoyed the mountain scenery, the sunrises and sunsets, the rushing, freezing-over creek. They realized how remote and unforgiving the terrain and weather could be. Wendel hiked through soreness; Mark changed to tennis shoes and would have walked until his feet fell off. Hunters like these are why I head for the woods each autumn. I am a people person, and there's no better way to get to know somebody than out in the bush where pretenses drop. Everybody farts, takes turns using the open-air outhouse (occasionally having to screech for a new roll of toilet paper), stays out of the tent when one or another takes a body odor-reducing spit-bath, and lives side by side with someone he or she didn't know days before.

When mid-August rolls around, some unknown force in me responds to the changing season. The cold breeze blowing through the open bedroom windows in my Fairbanks home will ruffle through my hair to cool my scalp.

"Y'know, Michael," I murmur to my husband as we lie curled snugly together with the quilt pulled to our chins, "this feels like hunting out of a spike camp. You know, under a tarp."

"I know. I was just thinking the same thing," he replies.

I lie silent, feeling a tug, an almost aching desire to be back in the freedom of hunting camp, trailing around like a gypsy. Could this feeling, this urge, be a throwback to prehistoric times, when people hunted and gathered in order to live? In truth, people have hunted continually across the ages, and for some it may be that the seasonal call is stronger, a siren song: "Come out, provide for yourself—help others provide for themselves."

Lying under the stars, shielded from rain by a tarp strung from the Bombardier to some trees, feeling the breeze in your hair while the rest of you is tucked in a toasty warm sleeping bag wrapping you like a cocoon, is a precious, treasured feeling. There are no tent or cabin walls to stop sounds or obscure your view. On moonless nights when the weather is clear, the stars twinkle white and silver in a midnight blue-black sky. The Milky Way cuts a swath across the heavens that's not visible from a town, where city lights fuzz the celestial view. The Big Dipper, Orion, the Little Dipper, and the North Star all become easy to pick out, and it's then that I wish I'd absorbed a little more astronomy along the way.

When the moon is full, the tall spruce trees, thick willows, and short dwarf birch bushes create stark shadows and patterns on the ground. You can easily see a nocturnal moose wandering by. And the northern lights, the Aurora Borealis! On your back in a sleeping bag is the best way I know of enjoying their undulating course across the wide sky-scape. Vivid greens, a shade of blue-green, and sometimes shades of fuschia, pink, and purple-pink grace the bottom of the riffling curtains that move along in sheets. Every now and then, I swear I can hear them, just like when I was a little girl and my parents would wake us up, bundle us in warm coats, and take us outdoors to see the northern lights. It seems nearly possible, if they came just a bit closer, to reach out and touch them. These are nights to treasure.

Wolves sing and howl, their voices scaling the register from bass to soprano, holding a low moan for an eternity and then reaching for a higher pitch. Several create a harmony. There are times when another pack from a miles-away hillside responds, and a song-fest carries on in earnest. Five or ten minutes go by as they

Camp in the Alphabet Hills, 1997: Mike Tinker and the author, waiting for breakfast. Photo by Helmut Ringlestein.

serenade us, then all falls silent until you nearly drop off to sleep. But a rolling moan begins the chorus again.

Sometimes you see once-in-a-lifetime things that you carry only in your memory. One of mine is of a swan and a cow moose.

One year, Tinker and I had Henry, a bowhunter, with us. At the end of a long day we had settled on a little knoll before heading back to camp. We were figuring out the best way back to camp—a return route up the hill or stay low to follow the creek—when we heard splashing noises from a small lake below us. Leaving our packs and cameras on the knoll, taking the bow and arrows and rifles, we crept down the small hill, hoping the wind wouldn't change and mess up our stalk. We weren't sure whether we would find a bull moose or a cow moose, but we needed to be ready. When we reached the lake, we had to stay nearly prone because there was no tree cover, only marshy ground and grass interspersed with short black spruce. The early evening clouds reflected white in the deep blue of the lake, and the setting sun imparted a warm glow, turning the grass golden and the scrubby spruce a soft green.

We found a lone cow moose and a solitary white swan sharing the lake. The two animals were feeding side by side, taking turns keeping a lookout. While the white swan disappeared under water to feed, the moose would stand, water up to her belly, watching the shoreline. When the swan bobbed up, the dark moose ducked her head under water, munching on grasses and lily pads. When she came up for air, water poured off her muzzle and ears, and grass sometimes draped across her nose. They were an unlikely and beautiful pair.

Swans usually mate for life, so this one must have lost its partner. The rut wasn't in full swing yet, which meant that the cow wasn't being pressured by bulls. They were so peaceful and such an unusual sight that it felt like a cardinal sin to disturb them. So we stayed until nearly dark watching the pair, not moving to get cameras.

When at last we did move, both the swan and the moose departed in a hasty rush of noise. We wished we could have stayed longer and not had to disturb their guard.

These are a few of the memories running through my mind, making me ache to be outdoors with the sky and the cool breezes and the sounds.

Alaska is my life-long home and I don't want to leave. No matter where I travel, what I need is here. Fewer people. Fewer restrictions, more unfettered country. Here, you can step behind a bush most anyplace to pee. Not so in D.C., Florida, or California. The hunting areas we work in are gems, marvelous microcosms of what Alaska has to offer. They hold a special beauty, a raw edge of untamed wildness coupled with peace, a comforting, healing quiet that gives me cherished respite from frantic work-a-day life. And there is a feeling of freedom that doesn't seem to exist anywhere else. I want our hunters to catch at least a glimpse of my home and its spirit.

I'm most at peace and have the most fun when I work with hunters like Musacchia and Dale Ruth and Wendel and Mark and others who enjoy and respect nature, for whom the application of skills required for a successful hunt and companionship with their friends and fellow hunters are more important than a huge trophy. Many are saddened by the actual kill. They count the hunting area as God's country. They come for esprit de corps, to share the time with people they enjoy, and just to be in the woods. They almost prefer not to pull the trigger or release the bow string.

These are the people who leave happy whether an animal is killed or not. These are the people a guide dreams of having in camp. These hunters don't care if I'm a woman or a man, only that I share their perspective on hunting and do my best in the field.

Most of my hunters? They fall squarely in this category, I'm pleased to say.

Mike Tinker (left) and John Musacchia in the Alphabet Hills in 1986.

Then there are less than a handful of hunters who are in a category of their own, who I would take home and keep if I could. To talk about one's best or most favorite hunters is an awkward thing, for there are many good hunters, and an equal number of very nice people. There are those few, however, who strike that extra chord deep down, becoming "personal bests." Or, to paraphrase G. Sitton, a field editor and writer for *Peterson's Hunting* magazine, you put memories of some adventures on the wall; other times you bring home trophies in your heart and head. Some of my hunters are definitely trophies in my heart and in my mind.

They share similar characteristics, even though they may be separated in age by nearly fifty years: a certainty of thought; sensitivity and good humor; practiced hunting skills; desire to get up early and hunt late; ability to fall asleep guilt-free in the midday sun; patience; confidence; enjoyment at being teased and a good joke; and a wonderful laugh. Two of my personal bests I met at the same time about twenty years ago: John Musacchia and Dale Ruth. John has left this world for other hunting pastures; Dale visits every now and then (he hunted

Richard Sallstrom and the author, 1996.

a few years ago with Wayne—my husband got to spend the night with them while I only heard their disembodied voices over the Bombardier radio). Another one is new only a year ago: Richard Sallstrom appeared out of the blue from Sweden. I thought the spirit and character embodied in John and Dale was of a different generation and possibly gone; Richard, who is about thirty, proved me wrong. I was supposed to be his guide, find him a moose and teach him things about the country (yes, he did go home with a moose, and yes, he learned a lot about the country and our style of hunting), but I think I got the better end of the bargain. Tall, bright-eyed, and full of wonder, he turned every day into a special occasion, making me smile and reminding me just how pleasurable a truly good hunt can be. It was as though Musacchia had found a new form and was visiting and Dale grew young again.

I think I'll keep guiding.

Endnotes

1   Alaskans often jokingly refer to the other contintental states as the "United States," the "Lower 48," or "America."

2   A Weasel is a tracked all-terrain vehicle developed and used by the military. Many Alaskans, particularly those in rural locations, find a variety of transportation and load-hauling uses for Weasels, one of which is hunting.

3   A witches' broom, called that because they are shaped somewhat like a broom that a witch would ride, is an abnormal group of closely bunched twigs at the end of a branch or at the top of a tree, typically caused by a virus or fungi. The most common witches' brooms in Alaska are found at the top of a spruce tree.

For the Musacchias: Barbara, Michelle, and John

The following was written several years ago by fellow guide Mike Tinker. Then, it was an introduction; today it is equally fitting as a farewell.

A Sportsman, A Hunter, A Friend

He's up before dawn and it takes a full half hour to run the chill out of the tent. No complaints, mind you, but I can tell he appreciates the hot cup of coffee. Seven days' stubble cover his chin and the strain of the hunt shows in the lines at the corners of his eyes. He sits on a wood and brown canvas cot, knees and hands near the woodstove.

It's mid-September and the hoped-for Indian summer has turned to driving rain, and overnight to ten inches of wet snow. More snow falls quietly from the dark sky.

As I stir the pancake batter, he pours another cup of coffee for each of us. We have hunted hard for seven days, guide and hunter, just us two. We are in the heart of Alaska's great Nelchina Basin. From the ridge above our tent camp we can see five mountain ranges in the clear air.

This hunter has been here before, not once but many times. It's a measure of the man and his dedication to his sport. He hunts the Alaska moose and grizzly.

Most hunters try to learn with each trip afield. If you are a long way from home with a guide who knows his stuff, you can learn a great deal. The guide learns too, each trip, each season, as the hunters come and go. He learns some hunters are nervous and apprehensive. They don't know how to measure their experience. Is there an overwhelming personal need to collect a trophy game animal? Does this hunter expect a bigger trophy than last time? How many chances can we get?

Sometimes the guide and hunter talk of these things. Too often, much is left unsaid. The guide evaluates each hunter, his ability, equipment, attitude, and fitness for the trip. How much can this hunter do on his own? How can I best help him reach his goal? Can I tell and show him enough in the short time we have? What is the measure of this man? For this hunter, am I a bodyguard? Servant? Master? Or friend?

My hunter gets up and stretches. He walks over to the tent flap and looks out. Just misses bumping his head on the lantern again. He is nearly twice my age, and the strain of the hunt has obviously tired him. Twice in the last week we have seen and stalked a monster bull moose. Every day we have seen the big bulls from a distance. As yet, he has not had a shot. I wonder how deeply he is discouraged.

He looks my way and with a grin he asks how much more of this "fun" we can stand. I know from experience and years of friendship that this man can stand whatever fate and the weather send our way. We have spent over forty nights in the field together talking about the hunt, families, hunting as an American tradition, and countless other topics.

We have walked a hundred miles, glassed four dozen canyons, and stalked moose and bear together. He appreciates the opportunity to be in this place at this time.

From where I sit, this man represents the good and positive ideals of sport hunting and being a sportsman. He has an unending sense of humor and many times has buoyed our sagging spirits until the strength returned to climb one more hill.

I feel fortunate to be his guide again. Over the years, he has learned the habits of our quarry. His eye is quick to spot the tiny flash of white on the far hillside that signals the big moose has finished his nap and is once again on his feet. This man cares about his quarry, himself, and me.

It's easy to enjoy yourself during the good times when everything is going well, but how many of us are dedicated enough to learn from and make the best of the tough times?

If you ever need a lift of spirit or renewed faith in being a sportsman, I can recommend a gentleman who can and will help. He is the hunter I have described and he is well known to most of you. He has the spirit, hunts with a longbow, and a truly fine sportsman. My friend the hunter is John Musacchia. You are fortunate if you know him.

Appendix I
Pass It On

TWO BIG-TICKET ITEMS cause me worry: whether my body will last, and why more women don't hunt. My body is something I can easily do something about, because it's only me and what I choose to do with myself in the way of exercise. Why more women don't hunt, why I don't see many in the field is a quandary that begs a greater solution than I alone can offer. Women don't seem to pay for guiding services, perhaps because of financial constraints or perhaps because they don't know how to hunt. So often, I've felt guilty because I don't get the opportunity to pass what I know on to other women; it seems that all the sharing happens with men. Not that sharing with men is bad; on the contrary, it's a gas. But I want there to be more like me out there pitting themselves against the elements and the wiliness of the game they hunt.

That my body will fail one day is a given, and I don't like it. After all, I go from desk jockey most of the year to heavy-duty, stretch-the-limits-of-your-body activity for a solid month or more. Lifting weights and tread milling during the year help. And in the winter I play women's city league basketball on a team that has been together for about twenty-five years, the core group of us anyway. That gives me good running time and a social hour too, since we often see each other only in the winter. We're an active group, and some of the women grew up in Alaska and also hunt. Basketball is how we stay in shape. Conditioning is something most guides stress when writing or talking to prospective clients: ya gotta be in good physical shape to hike where we have to go.

I found a partial answer to sharing my hunting skills: a program called Becoming an Outdoors-Woman (BOW for short). Or more correctly, BOW found me. Cathie Harms from Alaska Department of Fish and Game's Fairbanks office called me one day in late 1994, saying a number of people had given her my name as a good person for the organizing committee of a new venture ADF&G was kicking off.

"Oh, and what might that be?" I asked, not knowing what my casual question was about to spawn. Well, BOW was that new venture, and the first-ever

162   Walk Softly With Me

Alaskan session happened at Chena Hot Springs Resort the first weekend in August, 1995. Alaska's four sessions so far—one summer, two autumn, and one winter—have taught roughly four hundred women. A goodly number are repeats, with good reason, because in the two and a half days, each morning or afternoon has between five and six different sessions to choose from.

For women who want to learn, in totally hands-on fashion, about camping, outdoor cooking, fishing, shooting, big/small game and bird hunting, fly-tying, fly fishing, kayaking, packing for horseback trips, photography, gun safety, archery, snowshoeing, mountain biking, snowmobile safety, making firewood, chain saw safety, skin sewing, trapping, skinning, field-dressing big game, you name it, BOW is the place. And there's no lack of laughter, learning, and entertainment. Evenings are filled with outdoor and hunting clothing fashion shows; round-robin sessions of quick, special skills like knot-tying, plant identification, and animal track identification; goose- and moose-calling competitions; and educational talks on topics like safety in bear country.

BOW looks for instructors (women or men) who know their topic, who will make it hands-on, and who are people-friendly. I know: I've taught at three of Alaska's four clinics: for autumn, introduction to big-game hunting and field-dressing big game; for winter, taking your kids fishing. BOW is a huge door-opener, for both participants and instructors. Participants come away with the knowledge afforded by practical application, a whole new network of friends, and a boosted sense of self-confidence. Instructors come away with the special glow of having had a hand in a new awakening.

Sometimes, I don't know what I know until somebody asks questions. That's how it is with all the hunting, fishing, and outdoor things I do. I don't feel I know much until workshop participants start questioning me, then I realize: hey, there's a lot of important information hidden in the recesses of my head. I'm lucky that my family homesteaded, that I learned to hunt at a tender age, and that now I go guiding, spending about a month, sometimes six weeks, outdoors each autumn.

BOW has given me the humbling and exhilarating opportunity to pass on a lot of what I know to other women. It has made me articulate what I know, and be able to organize it into categories like animal habitat, animal behavior, physical conditioning, gear to carry, ethics, safety, shot placement, judging size, how to use a spotting scope, how to use binoculars, how to find an animal's body hidden in the broad expanse of a willow patch. Here, I can "guide" so many more women than one-on-one situations in a hunting camp would allow, should a female hunter ever have the wherewithal to get there. Women who've taken one of "my" sessions have come up to me in a store or at a subsequent clinic to say thank you, to share their experience, and to tell me that I am their role model. ("Role model" is scary stuff, especially when you don't know what you know.) They tell me that I seem so much like one of them that they really believe they, too, can hunt and dress game.

Gari Sisk, a nurse from Anchorage, took the first introduction to big-game hunting session, followed by a field-dressing big game session. She got so charged up that she went home and bought herself a rifle, a .375 H&H. Her first-ever hunt was for a Kodiak brown bear. On May 1, 1996, Gari bagged the seventh one she'd seen over a four-day period, with three shots at sixty yards. That brownie squared ten feet, seven inches, with a skull measurement of 30.2 inches. Needless to say, it scored in Boone and Crockett, and she was ecstatic. Her narrative for Boone and Crockett revealed the inspiration that BOW had given her, and she even mentioned my name. The photo she gave me of herself and that bear hide is very special. It reminds me that now a piece of me goes in the field with all the women who've been through my part of the workshops. Maybe I don't guide them in the sense that they're in the field with me as paying clients, but I surely helped them chart their path into the field by sharing what I know.

Look for one of the clinics in your state; contacting the Natural Resources or Fish and Game agency will get you hooked up. Or check the National BOW web page on the Internet at http://www.uwsp.edu/general/commun/bow. You'll learn that Christine L. Thomas, University of Wisconsin-Stevens Point, is the mother of BOW. Her research identified twenty-one barriers to women experiencing the outdoors; fourteen of those were because women had no natural available way to learn skills. What is boiled down to is that women weren't taking part in many outdoor, hunting, or fishing activities because of one primary barrier: nobody to teach them, nobody to be a mentor. So she developed and copyrighted a program that is equal thirds hunting, fishing, and nonconsumptive activity, presented by people who are experts at what they do. The program has three cardinal rules: no politics, have fun, and be safe.

My newest cardinal rule: "pass it on." Maybe I won't always be the lone woman in camp.

Gari Sisk with the bear she shot on Kodiak Island in 1996.

Appendix II
Field Dressing a Moose

Y OU'VE PULLED THE TRIGGER and your bull moose is lying on the ground. The realization dawns: you're responsible for removing the hide and guts from this giant mound that approaches a ton so the meat cools properly. You notice belatedly that one hind quarter is nearly the same size as you.

Where to begin? What to do first? Skinning gets the hide off, and from there on moose piecing is like cutting up a chicken. The moose, though, is ludicrously larger. Here's when you might appreciate having worked out in the months before the hunt.

The Five Main Steps

There are five basic parts to field dressing: preparation, skinning, gutting, piecing, and hanging the pieces or bags of boned-out meat. An experienced pair of hunters can field dress a moose in as little as an hour and a half. Three hours is average, and six hours isn't unusual if the animal falls awkwardly or in water. A word of caution: these directions are for the meat hunter. Trophy skinning is very different from the regular cleaning process and isn't covered here.

Getting Ready

Tools
    knife (one with about a six-inch blade and a sharp point)
    knife sharpener (Eze-lap is a good brand)
    small saw or axe
    thirty to forty feet of rope—nylon parachute cord works fine; I prefer halibut cord because it doesn't stretch.

Before Skinning

Be sure the animal is dead instead of just stunned or unconscious. Watch the rib cage carefully for signs of breathing, then use either your rifle or a long stick to touch the eyeball. It's a good idea to approach from some angle that will keep

165

you from being injured if the moose suddenly lunges to its feet, kicks, or tosses his antler-adorned head. This sounds dangerous, and it is. If the eyelid closes in response to your touch, look out. Your moose is still alive, and it's wise to discharge another round into the animal's head, below the ear and behind the eye.

Remove the brush around the moose so you don't scrape your knuckles and get slapped by branches as you work.

If you're by yourself, you may have to tie off a front or hind leg to a nearby tree or bush in order to keep it up off the ground and out of your way. You're fortunate if you have a partner. You can take turns holding legs up, pulling on the hide while the other is skinning, and work together to roll the moose over or move the head and neck to a better skinning position.

Skinning

Using your well-sharpened hunting knife, begin by cutting through the hide about three inches below the knee on the inside of any of the four legs. Slide the knife point under the hide and work from the underside out toward the hair. Trying to cut down through the hair will dull your knife so quickly that you'll spend all your time sharpening it.

Eventually you'll need to free the hide around the entire leg. Slit it on the inside of the leg as far past the knee and toward the body as possible. Then grip an edge of the hide and use the knife to start peeling it away. Use short, firm strokes, and be sure the sharp edge of the knife is away from you rather than toward you. Try to avoid slicing into the meat.

Since the moose generally falls on its side, I work on the bottom legs first, peeling as much of the hide away as its position allows. Then I do the same with the front and rear legs on the top side. Often, I prop its leg on my hip or upper thigh, which allows me to free the hide from the entire leg.

Many game regulations require that proof of sex remain attached to the bull moose. What that means is when you're skinning the hind legs, you must also skin the testicle sac, and then separate the testicles so that one remains with each hind quarter when the quarter is eventually removed from the body.

Once you've freed as much hide from the legs as you can, carefully slit it along the length of the belly. This can be done with your regular hunting knife or with a handy-dandy item called a "Wyoming Knife," a semi-circular, hooked device with two finger holes reminiscent of brass knuckles. It's blunted on the end that houses a razor blade, preventing accidental punctures of the gut bag and assuring a swift, uniform, and easy cut along the entire length of the stomach. Because moose hide dulls knife blades so quickly, some people even use the Wyoming Knife to slice the hide along the insides of the legs. While its razor blade only needs to be replaced once every couple of moose, your knife should have a sharpener touch-up about every half hour.

Begin the initial skinning cut somewhere along the belly mid-line. You can easily work both directions along the length of the belly, going between the front legs about ten inches up the neck in one direction and to the testicle sac in the other.

Once you've made the lengthwise slit, begin skinning the hide away from the body. Grip the hide's edge as you go, working the knife blade between meat and hide with short, smooth strokes. As you work higher on the body, you may find it convenient to slice hand-holes in the hide so you or your helper can get pulling leverage. Eventually you will have removed enough hide to bare the entire side of the moose.

Piecing

At this point you can remove the front and hind quarters. Have your partner lift the front leg as you slice through the tissue attaching the leg to the body along the shoulder blade. By following the front leg muscle contour where it attaches to the neck and to the back, you'll be able to cut through to the top of the back and remove the leg without wasting much meat. Your partner should pull gradually and steadily away from the animal as you make your cuts. Once the leg is off, rest it on some brush so air movement can cool the meat. Remember to do this with each piece.

The hind leg comes off in much the same way. Your partner lifts the leg as you follow the leg muscles where they attach to the back. It helps to think of the leg as a giant chicken drumstick—wiggling it back and forth helps you figure out where to cut. Slice down toward the backbone, angling toward the pelvic bone. If you've found the correct angle, you'll run your knife along the curve of the pelvic bone. Cut through the cartilage holding the ball joint and hip socket together, and then continue along the pelvic bone until you've reached the outer edge of the hind leg. As your partner keeps a steady pull away from you, cutting the hind leg away from the body doesn't require much effort.

If you're alone, you can readjust a rope to hold the hind leg up and away from the moose. You'll have a bit more trouble following the curve of the pelvic bone because the leg's weight will rest on the animal instead of being pulled up and away from it.

Some people prefer to remove the rib before "pulling" the guts. First, split the rib cage where the halves connect in front by cutting through the breastbone, or brisket. Slice through the meat from the ribs past the remaining front leg to the brisket where it joins the neck. Following that cut, use a hand-held meat saw (some people use an axe—I've always used a saw) and saw through the brisket. Second, determine where your rib cut will go. One method is to spread your fingers wide, then go two hand-widths down from the backbone at the rear of the ribs. Third, use a knife to sketch a cut line leading to the brisket, and then cut the meat between each rib. Now you have a line to follow with the saw, and sawing is easier because you don't have to push through soft meat. Fourth, while your partner keeps a steady hold on the rib cage, start at the rear of the ribs and saw through to the brisket. Lift the rib cage away and rest it on some brush so the air can do its cooling.

Gutting

After the two quarters and the rib section are off is a good time to "spill the guts." Using your hunting knife and extreme care, gently poke a hole through the skin and flank meat on the mid-line of the belly. At the soft part of the belly where the brisket ends and with the back of the knife toward the gut bag, carefully slice open the belly from front to rear along the mid-line you established earlier. Or, if you have a Wyoming Knife, use it—tuck the blunt end in the knife hole you've made, and pull the knife through from the brisket to the testes. This knife, engineered with a blunt business end and rounded backside to avoid accidental punctures of the gut bag, works very well.

The guts will bulge out through the opening you're making. That's both unavoidable and okay. Just push them back out of the way. If the top set of ribs is still on, reach up under the rib cage and cut through the flank meat that holds the gut bag to the ribs.

The next step is to cut the esophagus as far up inside the neck as you can reach. But before you cut, you should have about a five-foot length of rope ready. The rope has two purposes: one end tied around the esophagus prevents a wash of the green matter the moose has been eating from burping back out to spill over the fresh meat, and it provides pulling leverage for removing the guts from the body. Your partner will need to pull the esophagus and guts gradually away from the moose as you work along the backbone with your knife. Separate the gut bag from the animal along the backbone and from the ribs on the underside. As your partner pulls steadily on the rope, you'll probably have to push and shove at the guts to get them out of the way. Give special attention to the urinary tract and the anal canal. Don't slice the urinary tract (the penis should have been skinned and left attached to the flank meat and guts). The anal canal should be sliced off inside the pelvic bone.

If you're alone, it still helps to tie off the esophagus. You can use a longer piece of rope and cinch it to a bush to keep tension on the esophagus and gut bag as you cut. No two ways about it, though, you'll be faced with a lot of heaving, shoving, and pulling to get the guts out and away from the moose.

More Piecing

Now it's time to roll the moose over. Position the head so the antlers and neck won't bind you up as you and your partner lift and heave on the remaining front and hind legs. You may have to stop to reposition once or twice.

Once the moose is on its other side, skin the remainder of the animal and remove the hind and front legs and rib cage. The process will be easier this time—no guts are in the way and a good deal of bulk is gone.

After the hind leg is off, you'll notice that the pelvic bone is bare. With your saw or your axe, cut the bone off at the part of the pelvic girdle with the least amount of bone mass and nearest the back meat.

Then remove the back. Look at the underside, noting where the strips of meat along each side of the backbone end. Cut through the rib ends that stick out from each side of the backbone to mark your cutting spots, following with the saw to cut through the backbone. Take care with this piece—it's where your backstraps and tenderloins are. Visions of garlic-seasoned tenderloin wrapped in bacon, sizzling on the grill should dance in your head.

Now comes the cut that separates the hump from the neck. Following the curve of the hump toward the neck, slice into the lowest spot. Cut down toward the backbone. With luck, you'll be able to work your knife through the ligaments and cartilage that hold the vertebrae together. Or saw through the backbone once you've cut through all the meat.

With the hump out of the way, it's time to remove the head. Start three or four inches behind the ears, and cut through the meat to the backbone. Saw through the bone, and the head should be free.

Finally, antler removal. Skin away enough hide on the nose and the back of the head to allow you to saw (or chop) off the antlers. It's a good idea to have about five inches of the skull still attached to the front and the back of the antlers.

If you have to pack your moose, you should bone at least all the large pieces. Of course, you should do this only if you've brought game bags along.

Hang The Meat

Find a nearby spruce tree with long branches sturdy enough to hold the weight of one or two pieces of meat. I test the branches by grabbing on and hanging my 155-pound weight from them. Cut away the lower branches—the idea is to leave clearance between the bottom of the meat and the ground. If a tree with good branches isn't nearby, build a hanging pole. Cut a smaller spruce tree, remove its branches, and lash it between two supporting trees.

Then, with about a three-foot section of rope for each piece of meat, find good places on the bony pieces to tie one end of the ropes. On the legs, slice lengthwise through the ligaments near the knee joint, slide the rope through the hole, wrap it around the leg bone, and tie it to itself. On the ribs, cut a hole between the second and third ribs on either end, poke the rope through, and tie. On the back, neck, and hump, you'll have to finagle places at either end of the pieces. Sometimes you can poke holes through the vertebrae cartilage with your knife, shove-wiggle the rope through, and tie.

At the meat pole (or tree branches), tie the other end of the rope around the pole or branch. Be sure to hang any bags of boned meat.

If You'll Be In The Area Awhile

If you plan to be in the area for a few days and are interested in what other animals will do with the gut pile, there are two main things you can do. Gather up the easily moved pieces, like the lower legs and chunks of hide that you may have tossed aside, and add them to the guts. Pull the hide, fur side up, over the top of that pile and leave it. You may be able to see the spot with binoculars from some distant vantage point, or you may have to walk past the gut pile on your way somewhere. You will be able to figure out what size animal has been making use of the food you've left for them. If the hide is just a bit mussed up, your visitor is probably a fox; if it's pulled off, you could have a wolf or wolverine. If the hide is yards away and the gut pile is depleted, you have a bear.

Take a Break

Once all the meat is hanging, it's your turn for a breather. That is, after you've cleaned your hands and knife in a nearby creek or with the muskeg that's usually native to where moose hang out. Haul out your water bottle and whatever food you have in your day pack. It'll taste good, even if it's pilot bread shards and peanut butter. Be sure to drink about a quart of water, and then a few swallows more. Not only are you dehydrated from being out in the weather all day, you've also just been sweating from your exertion.

Now, stretch a bit and sit back (your day pack makes a good backrest), look slowly around at the result of your labor, and heave a sigh of relief. Your moose is in good shape, and so are you.

Appendix III
Hunter's Gear Lists

For a 10-day guided hunt:

Rifle (30.06 or larger)
Ammunition (two or three boxes of 20)
Binoculars (very necessary)
Knife
Sleeping bag (good to -10 degrees; a synthetic like Quallofill is better than down if it gets wet)
Day pack
Two pairs of boots—one leather, one rubber
Insoles for boots
Boot waterproofing
One pair light camp shoes
One pair wool pants
One heavy wool jacket
Two flannel shirts and two wool or fleece shirts
Four T-shirts
Three pairs jeans or similar pants
   (I've graduated to fleece)
Down, Quallofill, or other insulated vest
   (Primaloft is great; it packs small, stays warm when wet, and is the military's answer to down)
Baseball-style cap with sun visor
Knit hat (be sure it covers your ears)
One pair gloves and one pair wool mittens
Sturdy rain gear (pants or bib overalls and coat)
Six pairs wool socks
Six pairs cotton or synthetic liner socks
Two to three pairs of long johns
Six pairs underwear
Duffle bag(s) (suitcases don't fit in bush planes)
Camera & film (six rolls is often not enough)

Flashlight and extra batteries
Towel, washcloth, and shaving kit
Toothbrush and toothpaste
Personal first aid kit
Prescription medication
Chapstick
Hand cream
Book to read (good to have in case of bad weather)

For a backpack hunt:

You'll need to reduce the amount of clothing and decide to live in your clothes longer. In addition to the gear for a guided hunt, you'll need to add:

matches, plus another fire-starting device, such as a lighter or magnesium striker
first aid kit
cookpots
water bottle
small cookstove and fuel (I prefer the Whisperlite stove)
water purification means
toilet paper
food
energy bars
topographic maps of the hunting area

A note regarding clothing: stalking animals through Alaska brush must be done very quietly, so select your clothing with that in mind. Stiff canvas or slick nylon materials tend to be very noisy and reduce your chances for success. Wool is always a good choice, as are some of the new synthetics, like polar fleece. Well-washed jeans work also.

When selecting your gear, quality should be a primary consideration. It pays off when you're three hundred miles from civilization and really need your equipment. Your comfort, well-being, and hunt success sometimes depend on it.

Try to keep your guided hunt gear around a hundred pounds. Both it and you will be in a small bush plane for part of your trip, and it often has to be packed to your campsite, which could be a mile from a gravel bar airstrip.

If you're strictly backpacking, there are other considerations: your strength, conditioning, and the amount of gear and food you can safely carry. Backpack hunting trips are best done solo only by the most accomplished and practiced backpacker/hunters, and even then it's not the wisest thing to do. Sharing the load by splitting up the common but essential gear like a tent, cook pots, and food means you don't have to carry the whole camp yourself. Plus hunting with a partner is safer—another warm body in case you get hypothermic, someone to go for help if you break a leg, but best of all, someone to laugh with and to share the experience with.

Other Titles by Vanessapress

Vanessapress is the only press specializing in Alaska women writers. It is a community-based nonprofit organization, dedicated since 1984 to publishing the voices and dreams of Alaskan women. Vanessapress provides an outlet for women wishing to write about the Alaska experience from a woman's point of view. Vanessapress publishes works that reveal the courage, humor, humanity, and insights of women living the Alaskan challenge.

Titles by Vanessapress

O Rugged Land of Gold is an amazing and moving story of woman stranded alone and pregnant in the Alaska wilderness. Her husband fails to return from a trip, leaving her to give birth and survive a winter at their cabin, alone. Her story, and its happy ending, is hard to put down. 233 pages; $12.95.

Growing Up Stubborn at Gold Creek is Melody Erickson's second book about her childhood on a homestead in the Alaska bush in the 1960s. She and her family hunt and trap and face the heartbreak of a fire that leaves them homeless. "Melody Erickson serves up a hearty helping of both the savory and sad, garnishing the life of a young girl growing up on an Alaskan railbelt homestead" —Jay Hammond, former governor of Alaska. 212 pages; $9.95.

Bits of Ourselves: Women's Experiences with Cancer is an inspirational collection of journals, diaries, and poetry from women who have battled cancer or supported a friend or family member who has. A must-read for anyone in a similar situation. 152 pages; $7.95.

Karen Cauble was a barge cook on the Yukon River for a month in 1988. She salts *33 Days Hath September* with recipes and insight so that you enjoy this travel adventure cookbook and enjoy Alaska's Yukon River from a cook's point of view. 100 pages; $9.95.

One Post Farther North is "a collection of poems written sometimes in blood and sometimes with gritted teeth and sometimes with enchantment, but always with courage and openness" (Rev. Scott Fisher). Author R. J. Hodson writes powerfully and unsentimentally of life in Alaska. 57 pages; $9.95.

Tides of Morning is a collection of poems and short stories. Four Alaska women each look at freedom in their own ways, and each gives us a facinating glimpse of the regional flavor as well as the universal elements of their lives. 95 pages; $7.00.

Walk Softly With Me: Adventures of a Woman Big-Game Guide in Alaska, by Sharon McLeod-Everette, tells about the quintessential Alaskan experience—big game hunting—from the perspective of one of the few women guides. 184 pages; $17.00.

-- -- -- -- -- -- -- -- -- -- -- -- -- -- -- -- -- -- --

Order Form

Name: _____

Address: _____

_____

_____

City: _____ State: _____ Zip: _____

Book Title	# of Copies	Price Each	Total Price
Shipping and handling $2.50 for first book, .50 each book thereafter:			
		Total:	

Send a check or money order to:
Vanessapress
P.O. Box 82761
Fairbanks, AK 99708
USA